WICCAN
FENG SHUI

WICCAN FENG SHUI

HOW TO

ARRANGE A

MAGICKAL

LIFE

Alexandria

CITADEL PRESS
Kensington Publishing Corp.
www.kensingtonbooks.com

CITADEL PRESS books are published by

Kensington Publishing Corp.
850 Third Avenue
New York, NY 10022

Copyright © 2002 Alexandria

All Kensington titles, imprints, and distributed lines are available at special quantity discounts for bulk purchases for sales promotions, premiums, fund raising, educational, or institutional use. Special book excerpts or customized printings can also be created to fit specific needs. For details, write or phone the office of the Kensington special sales manager: Kensington Publishing Corp., 850 Third Avenue, New York, NY 10022, attn: Special Sales Department, phone 1-800-221-2647.

Citadel Press and the Citadel logo are trademarks of Kensington Publishing Corp.

First printing: February 2002

10   9   8   7   6   5   4   3   2   1

Printed in the United States of America

ISBN 0-8065-2296-8

Library of Congress Control Number: 2001098812

To my husband, Stephen, whose boot prints on my behind
enabled me to get this far.

I will love you 'til time and tides are through.

Contents

List of Figures

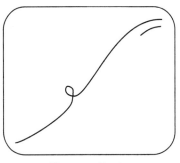

Figure 1. Begin

Preface

Riding the Dragon

If you had told me during the mid-1980s that I was going to become a Feng Shui practitioner, I would have laughed. I laughed a lot back then. I cried a lot, too, but that's another story. It was a time when I, like many others, was going through a spiritual revolution. (Or should I say, evolution?) I was no longer content with traditional forms of religion and was searching for more meaning in my life. Strange things were happening to me. Things I couldn't explain. Fortunately, I became friends with people who *could* explain these inexplicable happenings. As the old saying goes; When the student is ready, the teacher will appear.

One of those friends taught me how to meditate and stayed with me throughout my first deep trance experience. I was frightened because I had been hearing a voice and sensing a presence for several weeks prior to the trance. The thought of actually seeking out the source was terrifying. Visions of demonic possessions ran through my mind. (I know, I know, but I was inexperienced and Hollywood does an excellent job of brainwashing.) Anyway, it was during that meditation that I was introduced to my first spiritual guide, a young Native American woman. Hardly the demonic monster I was expecting.

During the following few months, my meditation skills sharpened and I learned to hear her without being in trance. She introduced me to other guides and because of her, I became convinced that the Native American path was the spiritual way for me. I attended sweat lodges and did research into the ways of the shaman and, although my interest in that path waned, I still have great respect for Native American ways. Those experiences were my stepping stones to Wicca.

In the midst of all this spiritual activity, I decided to meditate upon a new name. I assumed this new name would be Native American in origin and, quite frankly, still believed so until just recently. The name that came to me during that meditation so long ago was Dragon Rider. I didn't understand it even though I felt a great connection to it. It has (pardon the pun) reared its head from time to time, but never stayed for long. When it came time to choose a magickal name, Dragon Rider did not even cross my mind. Then later, when I became a High Priestess and had to, yet again, choose a new name, Dragon Rider was nowhere to be seen. Not even my coven name has a reference to dragons.

I had pretty much forgotten about it when, a few months ago, I was in a bookstore taking a break from writing *this* book. I opened a book called *Moon Time* (Paungger, 1995); a book on moon cycles, emanations, and so on. It opened to a chapter on dowsing and there, in black and white, leaping off the page was the name that came to me so long ago—Dragon Rider. According to that book, a Dragon Rider is a master in the art of Feng Shui! Talk about confirmation! The ancient Chinese believed that Chi (see Chapter 1) was the breath of the cosmic dragon and that those who could sense this breath and work with it—Feng Shui practitioners—were riding the dragon. Needless to say, I bought the book, brought it home, then promptly forgot about it.

I struggled with *this* book during that time, until that other book leapt off the shelf at me. Literally. I was moving a bookcase and *Moon Time* fell and opened to that page—the page of the Dragon Rider. Someone was definitely trying to tell me something! So here I am. Claiming the name Dragon Rider at last, embracing it fully, and taking you with me. Hang on and enjoy the ride!

The Magick Of Feng Shui

"Wicca isn't a religion. It's a way of life." These words were spoken to me by my husband in the mid-1980s. I had just found a coven to study with after several years of intensive spiritual searching. We had been dating about six months at the time and from what he could see, Wicca appeared to him as a philosophy—an approach to everyday living—and not as a structured religion. He was correct and incorrect at the same time. A habit of his which continues to confound me to this very day.

Wicca *is* a religion, but it is also a way of living everyday life with focus and conscious intent. By the constant and unrelenting examination of our lives, we Witches look for meaning in even the smallest of events and carefully phrase what we say for we know that words have Power. We acknowledge Power around us at all times and, through magick, we mold and shape that Power in our lives.

Wiccan Feng Shui (pronounced *FUNG SHWAY*) helps us in such a way that we cease the struggle to be balanced. At least in our homes. By bringing in all the elements and arranging them in specific ways, balance is created, and the effects on our souls are immediate and obvious. In our circles and in our rituals, we ask every element to be present, so why not in our daily lives? Most of us call upon certain elements when we work a spell or need something in our lives, so why not keep them present in our homes? In a physical sense in addition to a spiritual one. Moving furniture around or changing the color scheme in a room can completely change our perspective, both from a mundane and magickal point of view. Most of us have altars in our homes. Some of us have more than one. Why not make the entire house an altar space? By maximizing the flow of energy and balancing the elements, Wiccan Feng Shui transforms a reasonably comfortable home into an extraordinary place to live. By enhancing each area with items specific for that area, a natural harmony is created and our lives improve in every way.

In recent years there has been a growing interest in traditional Feng Shui. But that type of Feng Shui was created in the East and much of its tenets are based in that culture. This book differs from traditional Feng Shui books in that the philosophy of Feng Shui has been taken and modified to suit the beliefs, practices and philosophy of Wicca. If you have read other Feng Shui books, I ask you to remain open-minded. Some of what you find in this book will be contradictory to traditional Feng Shui, but I believe you will find this approach eminently more satisfying and in line with Wiccan philosophy. If you have not studied Feng Shui up until now, all the better. Writing is much easier to read on a clean blackboard than on one that has been written on over and over again. As you open this book, open your mind to all the possibilities.

Acknowledgments

I want to thank the Academy . . . whoops, wrong speech. Or is it? I used to think those speeches got a little carried away. After all, the winners were accepting an award based on *their* accomplishments. Right? Well, kind of. The creation of a book, like the making of a movie, is most definitely a team effort. Many people along the way helped shape the book you now hold in your hands and I would be remiss in not acknowledging those efforts.

Let's take care of business first. Thanks to my agent, Sara Camilli. Your undying faith in me over the years has helped me persevere even when it seemed I might never get published. Thank you for quieting my insecurities and don't worry Sara, I'll "keep writing." Thanks to Silver RavenWolf for being the first professional writer to tell me that my work was good and that I needed to find an agent to represent me. Thank you for referring me to yours!

To all the wonderful people at Citadel Press who worked on making this book beautiful, both inside and out. To my publisher, Bruce Bender, thank you for believing in this project. To my editor, Margaret Wolf, thank you for helping me to "talk gooder." Seriously, you smoothed the rough spots. I also want to thank you for enduring my endless questions. To all the others at Citadel Press whose names I do not know, thank you for being a part of this book.

Now on to the sappy, personal stuff. To my husband, Stephen Fishman, the list of thanks could fill an entire book, so let me "sum up." Thank you sweetheart, for believing in me. I couldn't have done it without your endless support and constant pushing. You can back off now. (Yeah, right.) To my sister, Lisa Payne, thank you for all your support. Your excitement in my accomplishments is a rare and beautiful thing, especially since you do not share my religious beliefs.

To my first spiritual teacher, Derek Fisher, thank you for opening my mind to a new world and exciting possibilities. Those first tentative steps, taken so long ago, were made easier by your confidence in me. Perhaps we will learn from each other again in the next life. To High Priestess Maeve and High Priest Arthur, thank you for teaching me the ways of Wicca and for being true friends. Maybe one day, you too will be able to come out of the "broom closet." To all my students, past, present, and those yet to come, thank you for teaching *me*.

There are too many friends to name them all here, but I wish to thank everyone who has believed in me over the years including the Houston, Texas pagan community, my soul brothers and sisters from the Council of Magickal Arts, and my non-magickally inclined friends and family. You know who you are! Blessed Be!

Last of all, I want to thank my mother, Barbara White. Thanks Mom, for raising me to have an open mind and not to judge others. Thank you for pushing me to investigate anything I questioned and for encouraging me in all of my endeavors. You have always believed in me and in my dreams. I love you.

Introduction

What Is Feng Shui?

The idea for this book hit me when I was contemplating buying a new house. My mother had incorporated Feng Shui into her home and had sworn to me that it made a huge difference in her life. With this in mind, I started doing my own research into the "ancient Chinese art of placement."

Feng Shui, literally translated, means Wind and Water. For centuries the Chinese have been building their homes and offices in harmony with the natural landscape and arranging their interiors to maximize that flow of energy. By placing structures where they are protected from, yet nurtured by the elements, the Chinese found a way to improve their lives. Something we, in the West, strive for.

Just as the first Feng Shui practitioners in China did and still do, we as Witches have turned to Nature as the Great Teacher. The fundamental belief behind Feng Shui is: If we live in harmony with the elements and invite Nature into our homes, our lives will improve.

Sound familiar? I thought so, too!

Being a Wiccan High Priestess, however, I immediately noticed fundamental differences in what I believe and practice and what traditional Feng Shui told me was correct. The most basic difference was in the elements. Earth. Water. Fire. Air. Spirit. These have always been the five elements in my tradition. In traditional eastern Feng Shui, the elements are Wood, Water, Fire, Metal, and Earth. Imagine my chagrin to find not only two new elements; Wood (which I consider to be part of Earth), and Metal (which to me is a combination of Earth and Fire), but no Air at all. How can you exist without Air? And what happened to Spirit? I can no more live my life without Spirit as I can without Air!

So I set out to create my own Feng Shui placement maps (known as Bagua maps). In so doing I discovered that I had been enhancing these areas of my life and home intuitively with the proper colors and items for many years. I had already been practicing Wiccan Feng Shui!

My tradition is a combination of Gardenarian and Dianic and the elements, directions, and so on are based on these traditions. I have also included bits and pieces of other traditions as well. I am beginning to believe that all American Witches, just like American people in general, are eclectic in nature. Pun, intended.

This book is written for those who are already practicing Witches. In other words, this book will not teach you Wicca. What it does is add another layer to the Wiccan belief system. Like icing on a cake, you must have a basis on which to build.

From the Fool to the World: Tarot and Feng Shui

Who put these tarot cards in my Wiccan Feng Shui? Who put Wiccan Feng Shui in my Tarot cards? Hey, they go great together! All right, so I paraphrased. The idea to include Tarot in this book came to me in the same way as most of my ideas.

It woke me out of a sound sleep at 3:15 in the morning. It was so insistent that I had to get out of bed and write it down. This happens to me frequently, so I wasn't surprised. What did surprise me was how effortlessly Tarot fit into the Wiccan Feng Shui philosophy.

You will find a Tarot trump or suit in every section of this book. I have been reading Tarot longer than I have been a practicing Witch and I find that the two complement each other extremely well. Although I use Tarot as a divination tool, I also see it as a way to gain greater insight into ourselves and the world around us.

You don't have to have any experience with Tarot in order to use it in Wiccan Feng Shui. Use your intuition. Buy a deck that calls to you and pull the card associated with the area on which you are working and study it. Since Tarot is so personal, I leave the choice of deck up to you. See all the images in the card. Where are your eyes drawn to? The bird in the air behind the main image? Follow that instinct and use a bird as your enhancement.

We enter this book as the Fool, standing on the edge of a great new adventure; joyful, but without the knowledge of how close we are to the edge of the cliff. We see the valley below us and the mountains in the distance, but are unsure how to reach them. Wiccan Feng Shui slowly draws you away from the cliff and shows you a beautiful path to follow. The World awaits you on that path. The path of Wiccan Feng Shui.

Enjoy *Wiccan Feng Shui,* and remember: magick is personal, so make sure to incorporate your own ideas as well as those from this book into your living spaces.

WICCAN
FENG SHUI

1

INSIDE OUT

The Tower

When we see the Tower in Tarot, we typically see destruction, but the more subtle meaning in this card is the clean slate that remains after all else has been destroyed. The Tower destroys even the foundation on which it stands, so that when rebuilt, your new Tower will stand straighter, taller, and stronger. Wiccan Feng Shui is the Tower, completely breaking down ideas about energy movement and decorating. A strange combination, you may think, and an idea that seems like fluff. I had the same feeling myself.

A crisis manifested itself when this book was about three-quarters finished. An insistent voice reared its ugly head and almost convinced me that what I was writing was pure fluff—designed only to make me money. It took several weeks of soul searching and long meditations to discover if that voice inside my head was correct or not. Since you are holding this book in your hand, I obviously decided to keep writing.

Decorating is *not* fluff, for the furniture, colors, and arrangements that we choose to surround ourselves with do indeed affect our everyday lives. That crisis was my Tower in this project. I had to completely destroy all preconceived notions called "decorating" and rebuild them from the ground up. That is what this section is all about, seeing decorating from a completely different point of view. Prepare yourself for a shock or two and get those sledgehammers and tools ready. It's time to tear down that old Tower and rebuild.

Chi

Feng Shui is all about the flow of Chi (pronounced CHEE or KEE). Chi is life force energy. Witches typically just use the word energy, but since this book will be talking about many different kinds of energy, the word Chi will be used to explain the ultimate life force, the energy that moves through our homes and our lives in a constant, steady stream. Feng Shui enhances the flow of Chi by using the arrangement of the objects in our lives in such a way that the flow is maximized.

Think of a river. It brings nourishment to our bodies and our crops. We can't live without a flow of water in our lives. If a group of beavers moves into the neighborhood upstream and builds a dam that blocks the river, not only will our crops die, so could we eventually if we didn't move on. But who wants to move every time there is a blockage in our lives? Use Feng Shui instead, because Feng Shui removes the dam or diverts the river and allows the water to flow freely again. Not only that, Feng Shui also guards the river in such a way that the water will never be blocked again.

The house in Figure 2 shows how Chi flows before Feng Shui, in through the front door and garage like an arrow. The

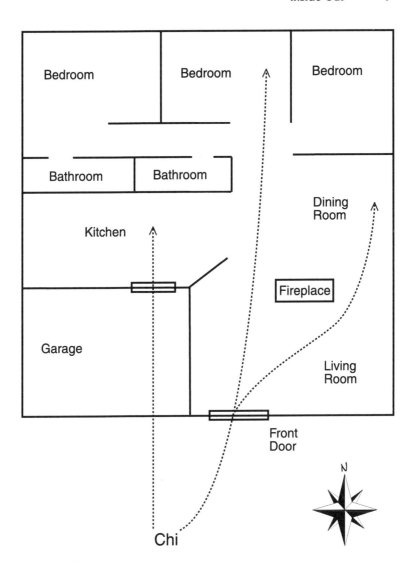

Figure 2. Chi Flow

fireplace stands like a boulder in the middle of a river diverting the stream. All the main rooms of the house have good Chi flow, but only the center bedroom is receiving that energy and both bathrooms are also neglected.

The following chapters will show you the tools you need to keep a constant stream of Chi flowing in your home through arrangement, diversion, or enhancement. At the end of this section, I'll show you a modified version of this same house with Feng Shui tools and remedies in place.

Yin/Yang: Goddess/God

Opposites attract.

It takes two to tango.

Those two are like night and day.

Clichés anyone?

The reason clichés become clichés is because they are so often true. In this instance, especially. One of the wonderful things about Witches is our acceptance of the fact of opposites.

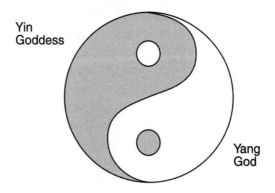

Figure 3. Yin/Yang

Most of us acknowledge the darker side of life, even exploring its paths on moonless nights. So the concept of Yin/Yang should be easy for us to grasp. You could even think of Yin as Goddess and Yang as God. Note that each carries within it a small piece of its opposite. This represents the philosophy of "it's always darkest before the dawn." In other words, when night is at it's deepest, dawn is on the horizon. There is another saying, "It is so Yin, it's almost Yang." The balance of Yin/Yang is easily tipped and when tipped, energies shift, meld, and transform. The small circles of opposites are a reminder of that delicate balance in energies.

The dance of opposites is a continuing one and although we would like to believe that there are no differences between male and female (other than the obvious external signs) we cling to this concept because it helps us define our world. There are no judgments here about what constitutes your goddesses and gods, only examples of the basic nature of female and male energies.

Yin/Goddess energy is dark, cool, and rounded like the inside of a cave. Yang/God energy is bright, warm, and angular like the rays of the sun. Both energies are needed in the home to help it feel balanced. If your home is too Yin, it may feel dark and close around you. While this is an excellent energy for a bedroom, it leaves a little bit to be desired in a living room.

Public rooms like the living room, dining room, and kitchen should tend more toward Yang—open, light, and spacious. Private rooms like bathrooms and bedrooms are considered Yin in nature and should be darker and smaller. Huge master suites, for example, may be beautiful to the eye, but are not conducive to a good night's sleep because of their Yang qualities.

If your living room is small and dark you can "Yang it up" by making sure there is enough light to fill the space. Furnish it in warm bright colors and sharp angular lines. Make it the most modern room in the house. Stay away from cool colors for they will only make you want to curl up in a corner and do nothing.

I will get more into specific rooms in Chapter 3. In the meantime, here are some general guidelines for Yin and Yang.

Yin	Yang
Goddess	God
Moon	Sun
Earth	Fire
Water	Air
Rounded	Angular
Shadow	Sunshine
Dark	Light
Cold	Warm
Soft	Hard
Small	Large
Wet	Dry
Night	Day
Winter	Summer
Autumn	Spring
Low	High
Silver	Gold
Widdershins	Deosil
Passive	Active
Receptive	Creative
Horizontal	Vertical
Ornate	Plain
Wide	Narrow
Floral	Geometrical
Pentacle	Sword
Chalice	Wand

Elements

As Witches, we work with the elements on a regular basis, so I won't spend a lot of time on definitions here. Just a short overview, then on with the show. It is in this arena that traditional Feng Shui differs the most from Wiccan Feng Shui. Since I want to keep this as simple as possible, I will not be making a comparison. I am only going to present the elements we, as Witches, work with. Earth, Water, Fire, and Air. Spirit permeates all of the elements so it will not be defined separately.

Each element has specific colors, stones, animals, musical instruments, and a variety of other items associated with it. These associations will be discussed in depth in the next chapter, as will the compass points of each element. This chapter is to show you how the elements interact with one another and with Yin/Yang.

All the elements reside within Yin/Yang completing the circle of life. All elements are present in us and in the world around us, just as each one of us also carries both male and female energies.

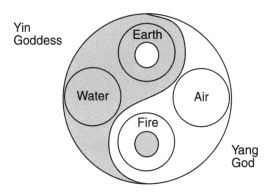

Figure 4. Elements

Earth resides entirely within Yin—Mother Nature, Gaia. Most of us see the Earth as female. Water is also considered feminine in nature—think of Mother Ocean and mermaids. Both are nurturing and healing, gentle and comforting, and cool and dark. Like the Mother's womb, Earth and Water hold us close to Her.

Fire is Yin. Father Sun. Keeper of the Flame. Most of us see Fire as male. Air is also considered masculine in nature. Mercury, the great communicator. Whirlwinds. Both are active and allusive. Both are warm and inspiring. Both are bright and open. Like our Father's hands, Fire and Air push us to succeed.

Just as deosil (clockwise) and widdershins (counterclockwise) circles are cast to achieve different results in our Workings, the elements interact differently when moving one way or another around the circle. It appears that one is positive and one negative, but I hesitate to use those terms. Rather, one is nurturing and the other one controlling.

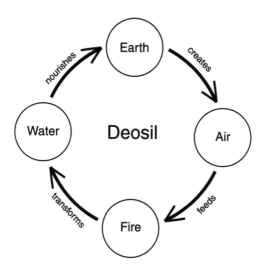

Figure 5. Nurturing Cycle

Deosil is the nurturing cycle. Air feeds Fire, for without oxygen a fire will eventually die out. Fire transforms Water, turning it to steam. Water nourishes Earth, encouraging plants to grow. Earth creates Air quite literally as the leaves of trees and other plants create the air we breathe.

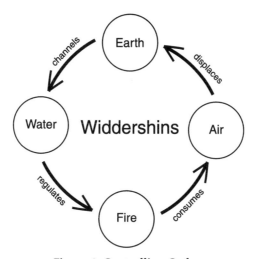

Figure 6. Controlling Cycle

Widdershins is the controlling cycle. Earth channels Water. We build dams and irrigation canals out of the earth so we may better use the Water around us. Water regulates Fire and can extinguish it. In the meantime, sparks flying out of a campfire ring can be easily put out with Water. Water keeps the Fire where it belongs, where *we* want it to be. Fire consumes Air and by so doing, burns brighter. Air displaces Earth by blowing the leaves off the trees in the fall and blowing away the dead grasses. It also ensures that new growth will happen in the spring by blowing seeds to areas where they can take root and grow.

Since all the elements are present in us, we need all these elements present in our homes.

Power Spots

Finding the power spots in our homes is a piece of cake for Witches since we are already sensitive to forces outside ourselves, but few of us actually take the time to locate these power spots. The best mundane way of locating power spots is to watch where guests sit when invited over. People are intuitively attracted to power spots in the home. Pets are also a good indicator. Does your cat love to sleep in the middle of the coffee table? Then that coffee table is most probably over a power spot. Consider placing your favorite chair there instead, so *you* can take advantage of it, too.

In general, power spots are places in each room where, when seated, you can see all the entrances to the room. We feel the most comfortable when in control of our environment and the best way to achieve that control is to know when someone enters or leaves a room.

The ultimate power spot in our homes is in the exact center of the house. If possible, hang a beautiful crystal chandelier in this spot and beneficial Chi will radiate outward to every area of the house. If a chandelier is not possible, try to enhance this area in some significant way. A favorite work of art or an item representing the goals of the residents brings the house alive and circulates good feelings throughout the structure.

A wonderful magickal way of locating power spots is to walk your entire house. Start at the front door and walk in a circular motion through every room eventually arriving back at your starting point. Whether you walk widdershins or deosil is up to you. Extend your senses and feel the energies. Take notes or, if it is difficult for you to write while in trance, simply drop pieces of paper in those spots as you find them. Even if blank, the paper will be over the power spot. Don't be surprised if you find yourself moving furniture the next day.

It is imperative that beds and desks are located in power spots, for you spend more time in these places than in any other. Especially if you work at home like I do. Chapter 3 will further guide you in enhancing individual rooms and taking advantage of power spots.

Lay Lines

Let us return once more to that river of energy called Chi. There are many of these rivers throughout our world, crisscrossing each other, coming together to form lakes of energy, and then dispersing again into smaller streams and canals. They flow constantly and, occasionally, like a river of water they will change their course. These rivers are called lay lines and if you are fortunate enough to choose the building site for your home, you can take full advantage of these forces.

As Witches, we can sense these lay lines easier than the average person. However, some are so subtle that it takes an experienced dowser to discover them. Some are slow moving while others are fast. Some are on the surface and some are deep underground, while still others are high above us. The animals know this too. Game trails in the forest typically follow lay lines. Major streets in most cities follow lay lines. Westheimer, here in Houston, follows an extremely powerful lay line and downtown Houston itself is one of those lakes I mentioned. Especially when it rains! Sorry, just a little humor to liven things up. Interestingly, most cities are built over lay lines, because people are instinctively attracted to the energy.

When looking for a house or a piece of property on which to build, be aware of lay lines on the land. While a smaller lay line may be beneficial, a larger or stronger one can be detrimental. It would be like building your house under a raging waterfall. It would be easy to get swept away.

Tools

The most important tool in Wiccan Feng Shui is your mind. Being able to visualize and imagine what you want to happen is the key to magickal workings. After all, spells are simply a way of focusing your mind, keeping it busy, as it were, so your spirit can do the work that is needed. Relying solely on a tool to do the work for you is a little like placing raw food on the stove without turning the burner on. It won't cook itself! It requires effort to make a great meal.

Being a practicing Witch, you will have many of the following tools on hand. Those that you do not have are easily obtainable. Remember, focus your intent as you use the tools and spells in this book and you'll be amazed at the results.

Athame

Your athame will be used in almost all the spells here, not only as a means of focusing energy, but also as a way of defining space. Your athame will also be used to activate the enhancements you choose to place in each area of your home.

Candles and Light

One of my first introductions to magick was candle magick, so there will be a great deal of that type of magick throughout this book. Candles not only provide light, but they are also wonderful tools for activation. The act of lighting a candle—calling forth Fire—is significant to our species. If every time you light a match you consider how many generations of humans had to strike flint to start a fire, your appreciation of so simple a process will turn to awe at the power of a single match.

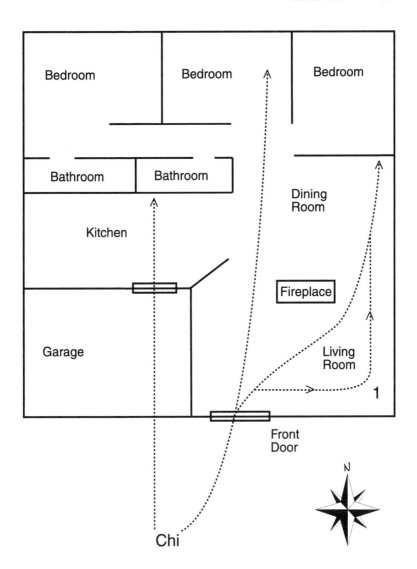

Figure 7. **Light as a Tool**

Mechanical light is also a tool in Wiccan Feng Shui. Where you place lighting in your home has an enormous impact on the people living there. Having enough light in our lives is essential to our well-being. Full spectrum light bulbs go a long way not only in enlivening our homes, but also in preventing diseases like SAD (seasonal affective disorder) from ruling our lives every winter.

The floor lamp in Figure 7 shows how light at area number 1 can pull Chi into a stagnate area yet keep the flow throughout the room. One note to add is that the Chi flowing through the house is not diminished by pulling some into a corner. The use of tools increases not only the flow, but also the amount of Chi in the room.

Mirrors

Mirrors not only reflect our images, but they also redirect the Chi flowing through our houses. Pay close attention to where you place mirrors in your home. If you have a mirror hung directly across from a door consider moving it, because it bounces the Chi right out of the room. If you don't want to move it try angling it slightly and the Chi will be encouraged to enter and circulate. The more mirrors in your home the better, with one exception—the bedroom. Keep mirrors to a minimum in bedrooms for mirrors are stimulating and your bedroom should be restful.

In Figure 8, notice that the entire wall (number 2) has been mirrored. This not only bounces the Chi around the room, but also symbolically doubles the amount of food on the table (see page 145).

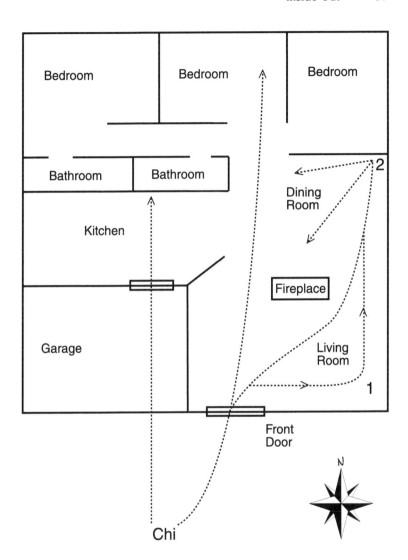

Figure 8. Mirrors as a Tool

Crystals

Another favorite subject of mine! With Wiccan Feng Shui, you should be specific in the types of crystals you use. Faceted crystal balls have long been a traditional Feng Shui tool. Hung in stagnant areas, they not only activate the Chi, but disperse it as well. With Wiccan Feng Shui, many different types of stones can be used. Details will be in the chapters that follow.

Crystals are especially useful in hallways, for their faceted nature distributes Chi in many different directions. Also appropriate in rooms where there are odd angles, crystals help the Chi find nooks and crannies otherwise hidden. (See Figure 9, number 3.)

Chimes and Wind Dancers

Chimes not only add a pleasing sound to a room, they also help the Chi to move, as do wind dancers and mobiles. There are so many wonderful, colorful flags with streamers available these days, that finding something to add movement to an area is as easy as picking up a catalog or walking into your local supermarket. Streaming ribbons are not just for Beltane anymore!

If you have an eastern area of a room that needs an enhancement, wind chimes and mobiles are perfect for they are closely associated with the element of Air. (See Figure 10, number 4.) The wind chimes in the eastern part of the bedroom are located directly under a vent, so when the air conditioner or heat kicks on, they sound beautiful. The mobile in the garage not only disperses Chi throughout the space, but it also greets me upon arriving home and helps me to judge where to stop the car, by lightly touching my windshield. Much better than the tennis balls I've seen elsewhere.

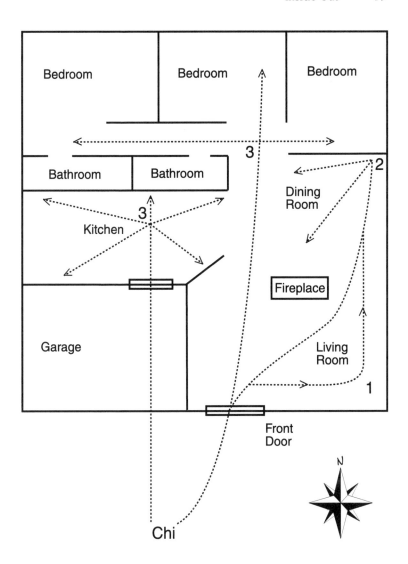

Figure 9. Crystals as a Tool

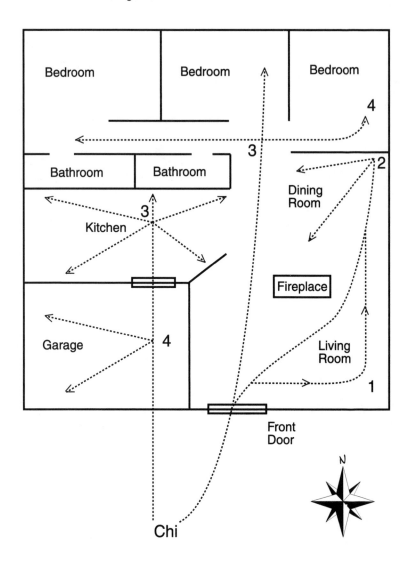

Figure 10. Chimes and Mobiles as Tools

Stillness

For areas that are too active, stillness can be achieved by placing objects in that area that slow down the Chi. A pot in a corner or a piece of art hung on a wall work well. Remember to keep the designs simple and still. A photo of a raging waterfall will do nothing to calm an area, but a statue of a sleeping woman will. Natural elements can also introduce stillness. A piece of driftwood can remind you of a gently flowing ocean instead of the crashing of waves.

Fountains

Here, once again, traditional Feng Shui and Wiccan Feng Shui differ. Traditional Feng Shui says that fountains are great enhancements and are good just about anywhere. In Wiccan Feng Shui they should be used only in areas associated with Water or Earth. If your front door faces South/Fire, a water fountain there might insult the fire elementals. And, trust me, you do not want an elemental mad at you. I know from personal experience.

As a matter of fact, when my husband and I were house hunting, we found a wonderful house that fit all our needs. The square footage was just right, the floor plan was perfect, and the location was convenient. It had one problem. The fireplace was on the West wall—the direction of Water. We decided to make an offer on the house anyway and maybe turn the fireplace into a water fountain. Well, we never got the chance. The house was taken off the market before we could make that offer. It seems that part of the foundation had to be jackhammered because of massive plumbing problems! Talk about upset elementals!

Life

Pets add so much happiness and joy to homes that, to me, a home without an animal companion is incomplete. Most Witches have familiars of one type or another, be it cat, dog, or snake. (Yes, I know someone that has a snake as a familiar.) Any live animal adds to the positive Chi running through your home. If you're a student living in a dorm or cannot have an animal living with you for any reason, representations of animals can be used as substitutes, although their power is substantially less. Instead of one live fish in a bowl, hang a mobile of wooden fish instead. They not only add movement, but they are also one of the animals associated with Water.

Houseplants also add life to your home by bringing the outdoors in and reminding us of all the life that surrounds us. If you have a black thumb, don't despair, silk plants can be used as substitutes as long as you remember to keep the leaves dusted. Again, the power is substantially less and you may find yourself having to add something else to the enhancement. Plants act in a similar way to faceted crystals in that they disperse Chi throughout the area in which they are placed.

The plants in the two bedrooms and bathrooms shown in Figure 11 as number 5, help keep the energy moving. They act in an additional way in the bathrooms by keeping the air fresh and to help keep the Chi from going down the drain (see page 158).

Colors

Colors specific to certain areas can be used not only to highlight a room, but also to help the Chi flow better. Remember that too much or not enough of any one color can tilt the scales out of balance.

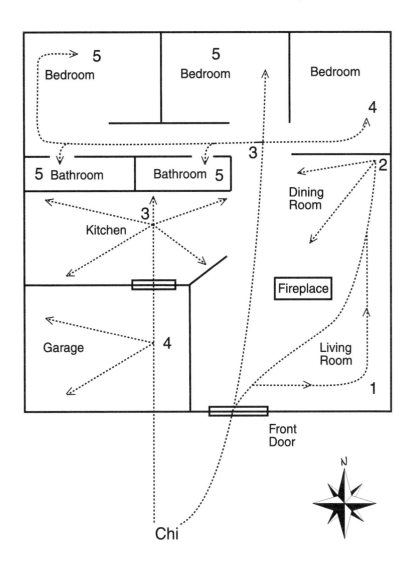

Figure 11. Plants as Tools

RED   Red is the color of passion. Red warms us through Fire, invigorates us through blood and moves us to action. Inspiration can be found in the red flames of Fire. Only when the metal is red hot can it be shaped and molded. The primal creative force is red. It is through the destuctive/creative force of fire that our homes are heated and our food is cooked. Red is the energy to begin.

Balanced		Out of Balance
Courage	Stimulation	Anger
Beginnings	Vitality	Violence
Physical	Manifesting	Dominance
strength	Intensity	Bluntness
Energy	Love	Wrath
Stamina	Bravery	Rage
Aggressiveness	Honesty	Grief
Passion	Vigor	Anxiety
Protection	Practicality	Fear
Sex	Decisiveness	Shame
Abundance	Vibrant	Greed
Survival	Fast	Inflated Ego
Safety	Masculine	Destruction
Activity	Risk	Brutality
		Suspicion
		Oppressiveness

ORANGE   Orange is the color of creation; creation *without* destruction. Sensual pleasures and gentle warmth reside within orange. Our fun, playful side comes out in orange. It is the color of fulfillment, friendship, and fun. Orange is a family picnic in the park during a warm summer day.

Balanced		*Out of Balance*
Creative	Stimulation	Shyness
energy	Spontaneity	Timidity
Attraction	Justice	Disorganization
Sensuality	Desire	Cowardice
Friendliness	Sex	Co-dependency
Optimism	Feminine	Dishonesty
Imagination	Joy	Overindulgence
Sensitivity	Enthusiasm	
Ambition	Social	
Happiness	Confidence	
Independence	Competitiveness	
Humor	Love	
Playfulness	Generosity	
Regeneration		

YELLOW   Yellow is the color of the noonday sun; the force in our galaxy that is the center of power. Its strength is gentle enough to grow flowers yet powerful enough to keep all the planets in our solar system from spinning out of control. Yellow is the color of understanding and balance.

Balanced		*Out of Balance*
Intellect	Hope	Controlling
Personal	Flexibility	Resentful
Power	Acceptance	Separate
Divination	Empowerment	Panic
Thought	Imagination	Perfectionism
Mind	Responsible	Detachment
Cheerfulness	Compatible	Judgmental
Memory	Fearless	Suspicious
Learning	Comprehension	Exaggeration
Fun	Confidence	Calculating
Simplicity	Sweetness	Skeptical
Balance	Trust	Secretive
Logic	Knowledge	Elusive
Optimism	Straightforward	Arrogant
Happiness	Joy	Intolerant
Relaxation	Ecstasy	

GREEN   Green is the color of the grass beneath our feet, the leaves above our heads and the well-being within our hearts; health, wealth and prosperity; the color of money. Green means fresh, still, and balanced.

Balanced		*Out of Balance*
Money	Harmony	Grief
Prosperity	Sensitivity	Loneliness
Employment	Self-control	Fighting with self
Growth	Adaptability	Materialistic
Balanced	Sympathy	Jealous
mental,	Comfort	Anxious
spiritual,	Organization	Greedy
and	Romance	Apathetic
physical	Contentment	Spiteful
health	Wholeness	Gossipy
Compassion	Affectionate	Possessiveness
Empathetic	Inspiring	Envious
Abundance	Cleansing	Moodiness
Fertility	Soothing	Controlling
Love	Relaxing	Paranoid
Understanding	Discriminating	

BLUE   Blue is soothing and calming. It stills the emotions and opens the mind to communication. Blue is floating in an endless sea staring at a cloudless sky, but beware the rogue wave that could overturn those lovely dreams. Remember to feel the currents beneath you and prepare for coming storms.

Balanced		*Out of Balance*
Dreams	Idealism	Suspicious
Calm	Centered	Critical
Peacefulness	Protective	Snobbish
Communication	Blissful	Scheming
Assuredness	Reserved	Cold
Patience	Quiet	Calculating
Consistency	Tranquil	Sarcastic
Spiritual	Personal Will	Insensitive
beginnings	Broad-minded	Patronizing
Inspiration	Faithful	Dogmatic
Wisdom	Tactful	Stubborn
Loyalty	Innovative	Ultra-
Contentment	Stable	conservative
		Self-righteous
		Inconsistent

INDIGO   Indigo is the deep blue of the night sky. Delving into this color lifts our minds to higher levels. Answers from both our higher selves and those that reside in that indigo sky are possible in this color.

Balanced		Out of Balance
Telepathy	Inner peace	Manipulation
Astral travel	Philosophical	Undisciplined
Past lives	Ordered thinking	Confusion
Charisma	Wise	Obsessiveness
Authority	Conscientious	Timid
Clarity	Kind	Impractical
Vision	Protective	Intolerant
Intuition	Unconventional	Passive
Fearlessness	Empathic	Addictive
Abstraction	Faithful	Self-centered
Spontaneity	Trusting	Introverted
Higher	Psychic	Remote
guidance	Higher self	
Understanding	Peace	
Insight	Self-sufficiency	

VIOLET   Violet is the color of the highest spirituality where all thought of physical and emotional desires no longer matter. To be secure in our beliefs and, at the same time, unsure of them is the grandest spiritual adventure of them all. All the answers at this level simply generate more questions. It is in the questioning that true contentment lies.

Balanced		*Out of Balance*
Highest spirituality	Self-sacrifice	Unrealized power
Meditation	Mysticism	Superior attitude
Royal	Fairness	Fanaticism
Divine	Charisma	Calculating
Hidden knowledge	Creativity	Exhibitionism
Power	Artistic	Destructiveness
Religion	Charming	Psychotic
Total release of material world	Transformation	Catatonic
Inspiration	Miracles	
	Transmutation	
	Self-realization	
	Eternity	
	Immortality	

WHITE   White is all colors combined. It is the center and beginning of a new plane of existence. It is togetherness. Wholeness. Completeness. Love and acceptance. White is the first step in our continuing evolution.

Balanced	*Out of Balance*
Wholeness	Emptiness

Star Runes

Dreams have always held great significance in my life. I can still remember dreams from my childhood as vividly as if they had occurred last night. When I discovered lucid dreaming in the mid-1980s (the ability to interact with and change dreams while still dreaming) the meanings of my dreams began to dawn on me and the information and guidance cleverly disguised as symbolism became clarified.

When the first Star Rune appeared to me in a dream on May 1, 1995, I took it in stride that although the meaning of the symbol was unknown to me, in time it would become clear. On the mornings that I awoke with a new symbol in my mind, it felt as though there was a band around my head. I came to think of this later as a "thinking cap." Although I don't remember seeing the Star Runes *during* my dreams, they were immediately clear upon awakening, but I found I had to draw them before I even got out of bed or they would disappear from my mind. I believe I was only a channel for the Star Runes—a way to get them to this planet.

The Star Runes like the ones on the following page are like letterhead. The first one represents the society that sent the message and the other three are the constellations closest to their planet. The society Star Rune (it originally appeared in gold) is the first one I received and it was a year later—to the day—that I received the star clusters. The Star Rune I have placed at the beginning of the book on page xv means "start transmission," whereas the Star Rune at the end, on page 212 means "end transmission this level," which implies there are more to come.

It was nearly five years after the first symbol appeared that definitions began to unfold. I was working on a new fiction

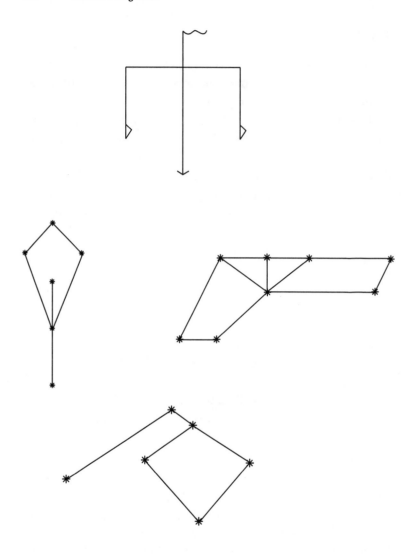

Figure 12. Society and Star Clusters

book connected to the crop circles phenomenon when, one night, I had a dream that the Star Runes and the crop circles were connected. The society responsible for the Star Runes is the same society that keyed the crop circles into our earth. They are an interplanetary group that can also travel between dimensions and are trying to help us through this dangerous time of chaos. The simple act of viewing these symbols opens parts of our minds and hearts that have been closed, and actually *using* the Star Runes accelerates the process, for our subconscious minds understand their greater depth and meaning. The Star Runes are like keys unlocking pathways in our minds, allowing new knowledge to enter.

The Star Runes appeared to me in three-dimensional forms that could be viewed from any angle. The meaning of each Star Rune shifts slightly depending on how and from which direction they are viewed, but since we are working in a two-dimensional medium (this book) I have included *all* of the definitions I received with each Star Rune. It is up to you to divine the orientation and, like with any tool, you may come up with additional definitions.

Like the Tarot, I found that the Star Runes fit effortlessly into Wiccan Feng Shui. Each area in your house has three Star Runes associated with it and they can be used in a variety of ways. They can be displayed, like Chinese characters, in frames and hung on the wall, a symbol can be carved into a candle, or a symbol can simply be traced in the air during the consecration of specific areas.

I have also included various Star Runes for different rooms in order to enhance the qualities of that room. Although the Star Runes in the Bagua areas are set for those areas, they are interchangable within the rooms. The suggestions I have made are the ones that make the most sense in my house and household interactions. Feel free to shuffle them around and change them to suit what you need in a specific room at a certain time.

The most powerful way to use the Star Runes is to meditate on one when you need what it represents. When you perform that meditation in a specific Bagua area and room, the effect can be spectacular.

Color has great significance in the interpretation of the Star Runes and the associated colors will be discussed in conjunction with individual Star Runes.

Please remember that the Star Runes can evoke strong emotional reactions. The words I have chosen merely scratch the surface of their true meanings. The more you work with the Star Runes and meditate upon them, the more the definitions will expand and deepen.

They are one of the keys to our next step of evolution. And before you ask, the answer is yes, I received all this information in my dreams.

Shars

"It's impolite to point." How many of us heard this phrase over and over from our mothers? Prepare yourself for a shocker. Mom was right. Not only is it impolite, it is bad Feng Shui.

A pointing corner in Feng Shui is called a shar. Shars come in all shapes and sizes and can make you feel uncomfortable, even unwelcome. Long straight lines are also bad Feng Shui. These are called poison arrows for the Chi flows as rapidly as an arrow along a straight line. If that arrow is being shot at your home, it can do quite a bit of damage to the energy. Walk the outside perimeter of your house and look for the following shars and poison arrows pointed at your house:

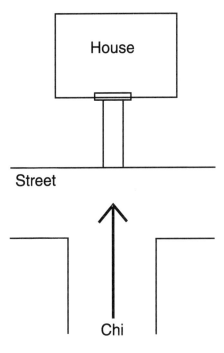

Figure 13. T Intersection

- The corner of a neighbor's house
- An angular roof line
- Fire hydrants
- Street lights
- Telephone poles
- Fence lines.

Even a street can be a poison arrow if you live at the end of a T intersection.

The best way to deal with shars and poison arrows is to hide them. If you can no longer see a pointing finger, it can no longer see you either. Hedges, trees, and plants are a natural way to obscure that line of sight. If that is not possible, then place a mirror that will reflect the shar back the way it came. Wind chimes also work for breaking up and slowing down fast moving Chi.

When we first moved into our new house, we started having minor plumbing problems (fire hydrant across the street), then some electrical problems (street light in the next-door neighbor's yard). I placed a set of windchimes next to the front door and performed the seperation spell found in the section "Kitchen—Heart of the Home," on page 138, and when I did the problems stopped.

Okay, let's go inside. There are shars and poison arrows inside your house as well:

- Table corners
- Fireplace hearths
- Kitchen counters.

Anything that juts out into the room can be considered a shar. Not only is it bad Feng Shui, but it can be dangerous. I have dived for many a toddler coming too close to the corner of a coffee table and while I was growing up, my hips were always bruised from a protruding breakfast bar in the kitchen. I have to be honest, I was a bit of a klutz, but still if that counter had been rounded off, well, I would probably have bigger hips today. On second thought, maybe that wasn't such a bad thing after all!

Seriously, watch out for shars and poison arrows in your house and try to arrange furniture in such a way that these hidden dangers are minimized. And make sure that no one is sitting in a chair with a finger pointing directly at them or they may not stay long.

Privacy

Good fences make good neighbors. No matter how friendly we are with our neighbors, we still need some distance. There is a lot of talk about personal space. I'm sure you have experienced someone who "invaded your space" or got too close for comfort. We tend to share only some aspects of ourselves with our friends, always holding part of ourselves back. This is called privacy.

In Feng Shui, privacy is an extremely important aspect. Just as we don't want to be physically close with everybody we meet, we also don't want just anybody looking inside our homes. Think of your home as an extension of your body, your personal space, and shield it from prying eyes. Drape your home like you drape your body in public. Clothe it and close it to the outside world.

I am not suggesting you shut yourself in your house and never open your curtains, but I am suggesting that you be discriminating in the times and ways you open your house to others. We all must go out in public sometime.

If you have children, it can be difficult to restrict who enters your home, but certain areas can be off limits, especially with a good lock in place! Personal space and privacy are most important in large families. Establish those spaces. Set bounderies, and relish your privacy, even if it is only a journal in a locked drawer or a hot bath behind a closed door.

Furniture

We need furniture. Logical. Straightforward. Furniture is such an everyday essential, that sometimes we forget it is even there. It gets comfortable and "broken in." Sometimes we have furniture because it was given to us. I have an old rocking chair that has been handed down for three generations and I love it! But a lot of us have furniture that we no longer love.

There is one basic rule in Feng Shui: surround yourselves with things that you love and those things will enrich your life. If you don't love it or use it, get rid of it. Every time you look at an object that you dislike, it affects your mood in a negative way. Sell it or give it away if it displeases you. If it is a family heirloom, give it to another family member. Keep nothing in your life that you do not love.

In youth, hand-me-down furniture is sometimes necessary in order to have any furniture at all. If you don't like the pattern of a sofa, throw a pretty sheet over it. If the color of a table makes you nauseous, well, paint is cheap! Find a way to make every piece of furniture yours, even if it means disguising it. Your home will be much more comfortable.

If you have hand-me-down furniture or if you love antiques, it is always a good idea to magickally clean them before putting them to use in your home. The easiest way is to smudge them with the smoke of sage and sweetgrass. If you feel that more is needed, then use all the elements to clean your new possession. Salt for Earth, Water for Water, A flame for Fire, and Smoke for Air. Using elements from your permanent altar is best for they are already consecrated. You can also ask a deity to bless the piece, depending on what it is and what you intend to use it for. A magickal cabinet can be consecrated to your personal Goddess or God, for example, or a bookcase to the great bard Taleisen, and so on. Pick dieties from your own personal Pantheon or find new dieties in books on mythology. There are some great books out there that have detailed correspondences. Specific consecrations will be included in each of the following chapters.

Remedies

Remedies and Spells. There really is no difference. One person's remedy is another person's spell. Remedies are ways to affect problem areas of your home when enhancement or redirection won't work.

Beams and Ceiling Fans

Architecturally, overhead beams can be quite stunning. In other cases, they are needed for support. Wiccan Feng Shui sees exposed beams as partial walls and the energy of these beams extends all the way to the floor. So if an overhead beam runs down the middle of your couch or, worse yet, your bed, you could feel alienated from your partner. If a beam cuts *across* your bed, your health could be negatively affected. Well, since we can't move beams, the next best thing is to make them disappear. Impossible, you say? Not for a Witch!

The following ritual can also be used for ceiling fans. Ceiling fans are a great way to help keep electric bills low (especially here in Texas), but they act in a similar way to exposed beams. Instead of a dividing wall however, you have a circular "cutting" motion. Ceiling fans can cause strife between the best of friends or seriously affect the health of anyone who sleeps under them. Make them disappear and you will feel so much better.

Invisibility Ritual

This ritual is best done in the middle of the night during a Dark Moon since what you're trying to do is make the beams disappear. By making them invisible you still receive the benefits of beams, but you remove the negatives.

TOOLS NEEDED:
Ladder (you must be able to touch the beam or
    ceiling fan with your athame)
Athame
Charcoal Incense Burner (with one or more of the
    following dried herbs): Chicory, Fern, Heliotrope,
    Mistletoe, Poppy seeds.

Prepare yourself as you would for any magickal working, and
prepare the space according to your traditions.

Invoke the God and Goddess of the house or choose a
God and Goddess of the night for their cloaking abilities.

Invoke the element of Air.

Light the charcoal and place the dried herb on it so it
smokes.

Using the ladder, get as close to the beam or ceiling fan
as possible. Saturate the beam (ceiling fan) with smoke
while saying the following:

Smoke create a screen
Between the room and these beams [blades].
Keep it [them] carefully unseen
For the safety of my dreams

After every inch of the beam has been passed over with
the smoke, touch the athame to the beam and say:

The structure of this beam [ceiling fan] remains true
Although it is removed from sight.
It is sturdy through and through
But gone is its negative bite

It is done!

So Mote It Be!

Thank the God and Goddess and thank Air.
The ritual is ended.

Mirrors and Glass

As Alice in Wonderland found out, mirrors can be doorways. Scrying is another way of looking beyond this reality and into others. What we sometimes fail to realize is that those realities can intrude upon this one, and just as we lock our doors at night, we need to lock our mirrors as well. Reflective surfaces in general should be sealed to prevent access to our homes. These surfaces not only include mirrors, but windows, glass-front china cabinets, and framed prints. This sounds like a lot of work and probably pretty paranoid, but it is a fairly simple spell and it is always "better to be safe than sorry."

Reflective Surfaces Ritual

This ritual is best done in the middle of the night during a Dark Moon since that is when the reflective properties of glass are at their strongest.

TOOLS NEEDED:
Athame
Black candle

Prepare yourself as you would for any magickal working, and prepare the space according to your traditions.

Invoke the God and Goddess of the house or choose a protective God and Goddess.

Light the black candle, and pass the athame three times through the flame in a widdershins circle while saying the following:

Blade of power, flame of night.
Remove my image from otherworldly sight.
Seal the surfaces touched with Power.
Privacy within this home will flower.

Move about your home in a widdershins motion, taking the candle with you and touching your athame to all reflective surfaces. Do this three times to make sure you have not left anything out. If you can see the candle's reflection in a surface, then seal that object.

Return to the altar, and say:

It is done!

So Mote It Be!

Thank the God and Goddess.
The ritual is ended.

Doors and Windows

The more obvious doorways into our homes are, well, doors. The previous ritual was to prevent otherworldly entry into our home and it can be modified slightly to a mundane protective spell. Change the wording to the following and touch all the doors and windows with your athame as you say:

Blade of power, Lord and Lady.
Protect my home from characters, shady.
Seal the surfaces touched with Power.
Safety within this home will flower.

The rest of the ritual remains the same.

Now that you have a working knowledge of some of the tools involved in Wiccan Feng Shui, let's take another look at our house. You'll notice that certain tools have been used to

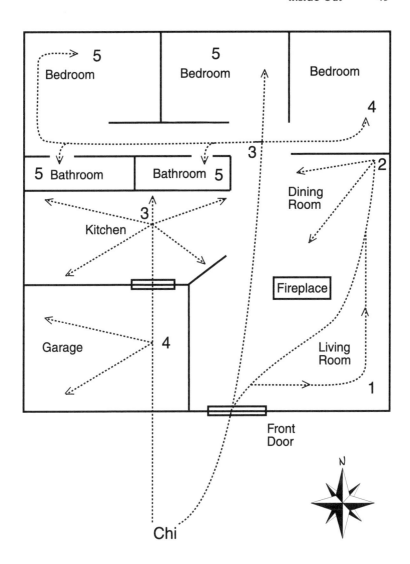

Figure 14. Modified Chi Flow

keep the Chi flowing gently around the living room, dining room, and kitchen. But now, the Chi is also diverted down the hall toward the bedrooms and bathrooms.

1. A floor lamp pulls Chi into a stagnant area.
2. The mirrored wall bounces Chi around the dining room.
3. Faceted crystals disperse Chi in every direction.
4. Wind chimes and mobiles circulate Chi throughout the room.
5. Live plants pull and circulate Chi into stagnant areas.

2

WHICH WAY IS NORTH?
BAGUA AREAS

*B*agua (pronounced *BAHGwah*). Strange word, isn't it? It sounds like I'm trying to tell you there's a bug in my water while my mouth is full (hopefully not full of a bug!). Bagua originated in the Chinese I Ching, or Book of Changes. This ancient text charted fundamental life issues and called this chart *Bagua*. In its basic sense, Bagua means the circle of life. Imagine a pie that has been cut into eight pieces and you have a Bagua map. Each slice is a different flavor (a different aspect of your life) joined together by a common crust. And just like you wouldn't put raisins into a chocolate cream pie and an apple pie is made with cinnamon, each of these areas has colors and objects specific to it. This section guides you through the "recipe" for each "slice," or Bagua area, of your home and provides suggestions on ways to enhance these areas.

A brief ritual is also included for each area. Please feel free to expand any or all of these suggestions since the more personal the rituals and enhancements are, the more comfortable you will feel in your home. So, if you don't like blueberry you can substitute rhubarb instead. Since all of my rituals (with rare exceptions) begin in the North, that's where we shall start.

Ever wonder why North is always designated on maps when, often, there are only arrows—or nothing at all—indicating the other directions? I know I did, until I began studying Wicca. It was then that I realized all things begin in the North, in the Earth. Seeds must be buried in the Earth before they can grow, Water then softens the shell and feeds the seed with its nurturing life-giving qualities. As the Fire of the sun warms the ground, the seed sprouts and begins its long struggle toward the source of that warmth until, finally, it breaks ground and feels Air upon its leaves for the first time. Eventually, new seeds will drop from this plant and the cycle will begin again.

Since both widdershins and deosil are present in our lives, they are present in this book. This section takes us widdershins, since that is the direction Mother Earth turns. It is also because of this movement that the Sun *appears* to move deosil. Our planets also circulate widdershins around the Sun.

It is this natural rhythm and the great circle of life upon which this section is based. Starting with Earth in the North and working our way widdershins around the Bagua circle, we follow this cycle.

The four tangible elements are located at each cardinal compass point: Earth in the North, Water in the West, Fire in the South, and Air in the East. The Bagua areas between these points share attributes of both the elements that bracket it. When all of the elements are brought together in harmony, the fifth element—Spirit (the crust that holds everything together)—manifests throughout the entire house.

I have modified the Bagua map from a circle into a square so it will be easier to lay it over a floor plan or correspond it to a room. This does not change the definitions.

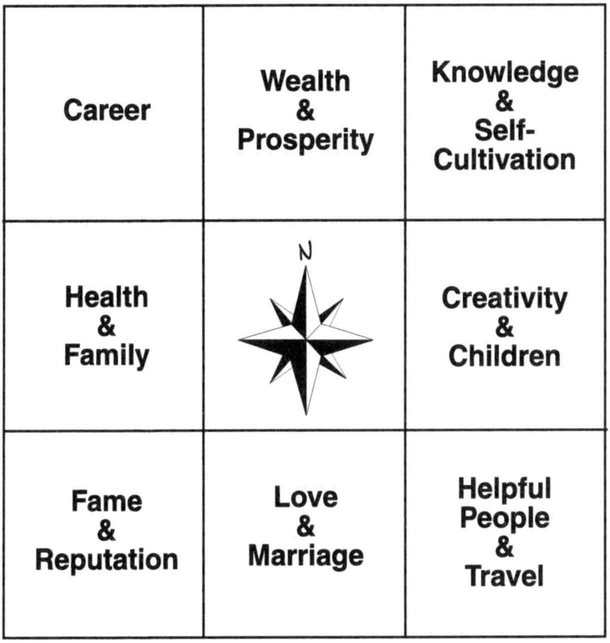

Career	Wealth & Prosperity	Knowledge & Self-Cultivation
Health & Family	N	Creativity & Children
Fame & Reputation	Love & Marriage	Helpful People & Travel

Figure 15. Bagua Map

As we go through each Bagua area, try to think of each enhancement as an altar whether the enhancement is as simple as a single feather or as all encompassing as the paint color on the wall.

Defining the Space

The ideal shape of a home is shaped like a pie, either round or octagonal. Yes, I know—round houses are not common in the marketplace. The next best thing is a perfect square or rectangle, like the map in figure 15, so that every Bagua area is represented equally. Okay. Better. There are lots of square houses. If you live in one of these—great. You can skip the next few paragraphs. If not, listen up.

Some homes are L-shaped or U-shaped, leaving vital Bagua areas out of your home. We don't want any missing pieces in our pie! Can you imagine a house without a Wealth and Prosperity or a Health and Family area? Well, neither can I.

By invoking the High Priest or High Priestess within you, you can define your space to include any missing areas. Traditional Feng Shui would have you complete the square with an object of some kind. This isn't very practical if you live in an apartment, for instance. But we're Witches! Wiccan Feng Shui allows us to morph our homes to include these missing areas.

The house in Figure 16 is missing the Health and Family Bagua area. If you lived in this house, you would find that, no matter how well you take care of yourself, you always have a cold or can't seem to shake a sinus infection. Since this area also rules family and friends, you might find yourself alienated from people close to you. You could be lonely for friendship or estranged from family members.

We fix this problem by defining the space. This is where your athame comes in. In the rest of this chapter and the next, you'll find specifics for each area. If you have a Bagua area missing from your house, read the section on that area, then perform the following ritual. The time of day and moon phase associated with that area is the best time for this ritual.

Defining Ritual

TOOLS NEEDED:
Athame
Representation of element taken from your main altar
     for the Bagua area that is missing.

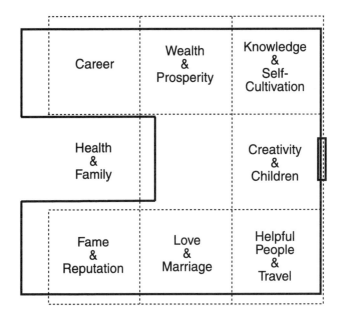

Figure 16. Missing Bagua Area

Prepare yourself as you would for any magickal working, and prepare the space according to your traditions.

Invoke the Goddess and God for that area.

Invoke the element(s) for that area.

Chant the following while your athame outlines the space to be represented by the missing Bagua area:

With this blade I carve this space.
A Bagua area I replace.
And seal within this sphere.
[Fill in name of Bagua area] be with me here.

Take the element or element(s) that belong to that area
and show it (them) its new home, and say:

It is done!

So Mote It Be!

Thank the Goddess and God and the element. You can
now decorate the area accordingly.
The ritual is ended.

There. Doesn't that look better? (See Figure 17.) The size
of each Bagua area matters less than having each area represented. As long as your enhancements hold Power, that area of
your life will flourish. Notice that the exact center of your house
has moved. Remember that when you enhance the center of
your house.

Now that all the Bagua areas in your house are defined—
missing or not—it is time to enhance each area. Remember, you
are the High Priest or High Priestess of your life and of the
Bagua areas. Take this Power and explore. Have fun!

The Quarters

We start enhancing our Bagua areas with the Quarters, by
moving through each of the four Quarters and elements. Then
we will spiral in again with the Cross-Quarters eventually

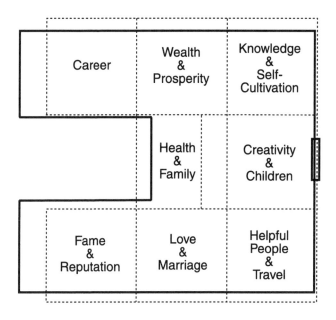

Figure 17. Modified Bagua Area

making two full circles. The Quarters represent the basic elements both in nature and in our homes and relate directly to the home and the areas in your life that are the most personal and private. We must have the square, solid foundation of Wealth and Prosperity, Health and Family, Love and Marriage, and Creativity and Children to make our homes complete before venturing out into the Cross-Quarter Bagua areas of Career, Fame and Reputation, Helpful People and Travel, and Knowledge and Self-Cultivation.

North—Wealth and Prosperity

Imagine lying on a thick carpet of freshly mown grass. You smell the richness of the soil beneath you as you stare through a canopy of vivid green leaves. Shifting slightly, you're brought out of your daydream by a sharp rock poking you in the ribs. Oh, well. Nothing's perfect. But if you move that rock, you can lie down once again and be much more comfortable. Wiccan Feng Shui moves the rock out from beneath you, places it where it will not be stumbled over, and displays it so it can be appreciated for its unique beauty. The grass, soil, leaves, and rock all belong to the element of Earth.

Due North is the Bagua area of Wealth and Prosperity. The first thing that springs to mind is money and, although monetary wealth *is* a prime consideration of this area, the definition of Wealth and Prosperity goes much further than that. One can be wealthy in friends and prosperous in love. An intellectual person is said to contain "a wealth of knowledge." A prosperous creative drive could find you with a house full of your own paintings even if you never try to sell them.

Since we want Wealth and Prosperity to grow in our lives, the most common enhancement to this area is a large healthy houseplant or a small tree. Make sure you keep the dead leaves trimmed off and nip any infestation in the bud. Ceramic or earthenware pots as well as iron planters with designs matching your goals are excellent vessels for any plant in this area. Look to the Celts or Druids for information on the magickal properties of trees and plants. Since there are entire books dedicated to this subject, I'll give you only one example. To enable you to better see future issues involving Wealth and Prosperity or if you have just begun a long-term savings plan, place a pine tree in the North for foresight and new beginnings.

Don't despair if you have a black thumb because there are other, less obvious ways to enhance this area. If you want to stay with the Earth theme, a painting of a forest scene or a silk plant will do. Whether you use a silk plant or a real one, remember to keep the leaves dusted in order to keep the Chi flowing easily. A rock garden or Chinese Zen garden is also good in this area, especially if you occasionally rearrange the stones. Periodic change helps keep our perspectives fresh.

Away from the Earth theme, anything that you consider a symbol of wealth is a good enhancement. For example, if the Wealth and Prosperity Bagua area is in your bedroom, you could place your jewelry box in the North or that special figurine that you just couldn't live without. A change jar definitely keeps your wealth growing because those nickels and dimes are representative of greater wealth. To increase the magick of a change jar, drop a piece of jade or malachite into the jar along with the coins. Jade is a great stone for clarity of purpose, something you need when it comes to wealth. It also sharpens your judgment skills so you may find yourself being less frivolous with your money. Malachite embodies the true essence of Earth with its dark green lines and overall rich green color. It is a stone that adds joy to whatever it touches—a good thing when it comes to money! When it comes time to cash in your change, leave the stone and at least one coin in the jar as seed money and watch your wealth increase once again.

CRYSTALS. A large green aventurine placed here will help remove any emotional blocks you may have concerning wealth and prosperity. This stone breaks limitations, sweeps away outmoded behavior and opens up greater possibilities.

ANIMALS.   Living creatures are especially good Feng Shui because their life force helps keep the Chi flowing. When you have animals in a Bagua area, make sure other enhancements are present as well to keep the energy strong when the animals are out of their cages.

If you have a small pet such as a hamster or mouse, the northern area of the house is a good place for their home because these creatures are sly and unobtrusive about achieving their wealth. Dogs and horses are also creatures that belong to the Earth so Fido's bed or a photo of Black Beauty would also be appropriate. Dogs represent loyalty and are highly protective of their home and pack and horses have forever been a symbol of wealth. Horses are also closely associated with the land and the Goddess. Who could ever forget Epona?

The cow is also a good animal for this area. Everywhere I look, there are cows or spotted furniture to make it look like a cow. If you have an affinity for cows or cow stuff, consider placing it in the North. The cow is yet another representation of the Goddess and brings nourishment into our homes. Bulls are a more potent symbol of wealth. The bear is closely associated with Earth for many reasons. She spends her winter buried deep within the warmth of the Earth. Her star, known as the Great Bear, shines the brightest at the Winter Solstice and her strength and power are undeniable.

The most powerful animal associated with the North, however, is the stag. His fierce independence gives us the pride and strength we need to pursue wealth and prosperity, so place any antlers or antler crown you may have in this area.

MUSICAL INSTRUMENTS.   We all know that there's nothing like a good drumming circle to get energy moving. If you are a Witch that just loves to drum, store your drum and percussion instruments in the North. The power inherent in a drum used for magickal purposes is a potent symbol of Earth energy.

AGE.   Since the North is also representative of old age, your grandmother's rocking chair could live in the North. Not only is the chair itself old, its presence reminds us of our ancestors and the wealth of love they have bestowed upon us over the years. Any family heirloom or antique wood furniture is appropriate here, but only if it carries happy memories. If it is a reminder of hard times, store it elsewhere or, better yet, pass it on to another family member who has more positive memories associated with it. In general, Feng Shui works best when we surround ourselves with *only* those items that are reminders of joyful times.

HOLIDAYS.   Sledding. Snow skiing. Trees covered with snow. Getting cold yet? No? Frozen ponds. Ice Skating. Wool mittens. How about now? Still not? Okay . . . Goose down comforters. Polar bears. Northern lights. Aha! North—land of snow and ice. Land of winter! A seasonal altar is something I keep on my mantle throughout the year, but I always try to place a little something extra in the Bagua area that is associated with the current season. A lone pinecone sitting next to my jewelry box during the winter adds a little extra sparkle to the season. It is also a constant reminder of new beginnings during the long dark nights of winter. Placing your Yule Log in the northern part of your living room means placing it in its position of honor, thus reinforcing the magick of the season.

TIME OF DAY/MOON CYCLE.   Just as the Winter Solstice is the dark part of our year, midnight is the dark part of our day, and so it is the time of day associated with the North. When there is no moon in the sky we can better see the stars, so darkness is

not something to be feared, but explored. The intricacy of the
night sky is revealed when the Goddess Selene leaves the sky to
visit her human lover. The dark of the moon is a time of rest-
ing our eyes and seeing beyond the obvious.

COLOR.   Green is not only the color of money and living
plants; it is also the color of empathy. Be practical about your
wealth, but *feel* what should be done with it as well. Feel for
other people's needs and give some of your excess prosperity
away, even if it is only a sweater you have outgrown. The color
green centered over our hearts reminds us to share the wealth.

STAR RUNES.   The Star Runes opposite should be viewed in the
color green either by copying them onto green paper or by tracing the actual symbol in green.

NUMBERS.   The most solid foundational structure is one with
four equally spaced points; a square. We must have wealth and
prosperity as the foundation in our lives—the surface on which
to build. Group Four of any of the previously discussed items
and you reinforce the power of Earth.

TAROT.   The Tarot suit of Pentacles belongs in the North. Not
only are they representative of Earth, but of Wealth and Prosperity as well. I live in Texas and our state symbol is a five
pointed star. Pretty cool, huh? Since we are called the Lone Star
State, antique stores here carry a plethora of old iron stars that
once adorned railroad stations and other "official" state buildings. These are great enhancements! Not only do they represent
the North, but also my faith and my state! Scout around, you'll
be surprised at some of the places you can find pentacles.

The Earth is about all things physical and material in our
lives. By enhancing this area we stabilize our world.

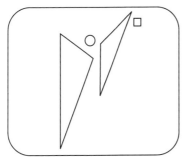

Figure 18. Health, Emotional Strength

Physical health is the best path to emotional strength. This Star Rune is a reminder that true wealth is achieved only when mind, body, and spirit are in balance.

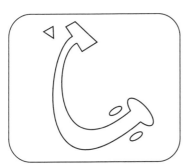

Figure 19. Self Love, Going Within, Inner Quiet

We must have self-love in order to give love to others. Only by going within and finding the dance within the stillness can we achieve the inner quiet that is vital to love. All prosperity must be found within before it can be achieved without.

Figure 20. Physical Strength, Motherhood, Goddess Energy, Balance of Opposites, Relationships With Women

To become a mother is to balance the apparent opposites of physical strength (worldly pursuits) with Goddess energy (spiritual and creative pursuits) thereby giving birth to all things possible. Our hopes and dreams must be planted within Mother Earth before they can grow into Wealth and Prosperity.

Consecration Ritual

Once you have chosen the enhancements for your Wealth and Prosperity Bagua area, you will want to perform the following ritual to consecrate those items. This ritual is best done at midnight during the dark of the moon, since that is the time of day and moon cycle associated with the North.

YOU WILL NEED:
Your athame
The saucer of salt from your main altar
A green candle

Choose a Goddess and God associated with the Earth, forests, North, or Winter. I am presenting this ritual with Artemis and Cernunnos, but please feel free to change these to deities you work well with.

Prepare yourself as you would for any magickal working, and prepare the space according to your traditions.

Facing due North, invoke the Goddess and God asking them to be with you as you consecrate these sacred items.

Artemis, Goddess of forests and wild creatures.
Be with me to bless and consecrate these items so that they
   may keep this dwelling alive with the power of the forest
   and fields.

So Mote It Be!

Cernunnos, God of the Hunt, Great Stag.
Be with me to bless and consecrate these items so that they
   may keep this dwelling alive with the power of the forest
   and fields.

So Mote It Be!

Light the green candle.

Call the element of North to be present in the candle and the salt as you touch your athame to each in turn, and say:

Guardians of the North
Powers of Earth
Be with me to bless and consecrate these items so that they
    may keep this dwelling alive with the power of the forest
    and fields.

The light of your strength, stability, fertility, and growth
    permeates this _____ [touch athame to chosen
    enhancements].
Burn bright in my home for now and evermore.

Sprinkle salt on the enhancements, and say:

I bless and consecrate these items with the salt of the Earth.
May Wealth and Prosperity reign within my home.

So Mote It Be!

Thank you Guardians of the North,
Powers of Earth.
Go in Peace.

Thank you Artemis,
Go in Peace.

Thank you Cernunnos,
Go in Peace.

It is done!

Let the candle burn until it goes out on its own. Your Bagua area of Wealth and Prosperity is now set.

The ritual is ended.

Magickal Workings

Now that the Wealth and Prosperity area of your home is consecrated, you may wish to perform certain rituals or place specific items in this area that relate to wealth and prosperity. You can choose something from the list below, or add your own suggestions in the space provided.

Rituals for:
Abundance
Strength
Fertility problems
Money issues
Grounding
General stability
Prosperity

Items:
Photos of things you desire
Your wallet or purse
A garage sale sign (before
    posting it)

My ideas:

West—Health and Family

Imagine floating in the ocean on a sparkling day surrounded by the people closest to you. By dipping your foot or hand beneath the surface, you feel the currents under you. A crab decides you're in its way and nips at your toe, but only slightly. You feel the tail fin of a fish swim by and you feel totally relaxed and at peace drifting with the ebb and flow of the waves. Suddenly a large wave knocks you over and you come up sputtering. Your friends in the water around you show concern until they are certain that you are okay and you all share a good laugh. If you had been a little more aware of your surroundings perhaps you could have ridden the wave in and used its power to your benefit instead of being overwhelmed by it. Wiccan Feng Shui provides a raft to safely ride those waves and a rudder to test the currents beneath you. Water is the element of the West and its color is that of the deepest ocean—indigo blue.

Due West is the Bagua area of Health and Family. These two issues form a symbiotic relationship to one another. When we're healthy we tend to be more active, thereby attracting new friends and enjoying time spent with our families. As the circle comes around, good relationships with family and friends improve our general well-being. The broad definition of family applies here, including close friends and neighbors and health refers to all aspects of health: physical, emotional, spiritual, and mental.

Since we want health and family to flow smoothly in our lives, the most common enhancement to this area is a water fountain. There are such a wide array of small fountains to choose from in today's marketplace that you can easily find one to fit your lifestyle and budget. You can fill it with rocks gathered from your favorite hiking trail, special crystals, or (if it's big enough) fish and water lilies. Some of the more recent introductions include a candle with the fountain. NOT a good idea. Fire and water don't mix and the Chi gets very confused if you try to combine them. For the same reason I strongly discourage the use of floating candles in vases, pools, fountains, and so on. Keep the fire *out* of the water and on the shore where it belongs. Besides, Fire reflected *in* water is a much more pleasing effect than Fire *on* the water. Remember to keep the water fresh and clean. Stagnant water slows down and clogs up our health.

If you don't have or don't want a fountain in your home, anything from the sea is appropriate: a basketful of shells, a starfish, or a piece of driftwood will work nicely. Keep the lines soft and flowing by putting sheers or drapes on western windows as opposed to miniblinds or a rolling shade. Live plants keep the Chi flowing in all areas of your house, not just the North. For the West, choose plants that are intrinsically connected to water like Aloe Vera (see page 137) or Catnip for beauty and happiness. Your cat will love you for it! For fresh cut flowers try Daisies for love; Violets for protection, wishes, and peace; or Gardenias for healing and spirituality. Remember to change the water frequently and pull out wilting flowers. Never allow dead flowers to remain in your home, especially in the Health area or you will find your health suffering as a result.

METALS.   I have a copper gelatin mold in the shape of a fish that I have hung in the West. The obvious enhancement here is the fish. The less obvious enhancement is the material, copper. Along with silver, these two metals belong in the West, so if you have a beautiful silver platter that you want to show off, put it on a West wall and keep it polished!

CRYSTALS.   Lapis, blue fluorite, sodalite, and sugilite are good additions to this area. The deep blue of lapis reminds us of the sea while it encourages deep meditation and the gold flecks within the stone show us the golden light of divinity. If you are having difficulty communicating with the people closest to you, sodalite can help break that barrier. Great health comes from the silence within and puts us in touch with our own divinity.

ANIMALS.   If you have an aquarium, keep it in the West. Fish love it in the West and it is no coincidence that fish are also very healthy to eat. Photos or statues of marine animals are appropriate here including whales and dolphins. There is one school of thought that says whales and dolphins were human at one time and that the next stage of our evolution is the next step to becoming these playful, social creatures. Whales and dolphins also remind us that we must remember to take time to play if we want total health.

The most surprising animal connected to water is the cat. That's right, I said the cat. It's a common cliché that cats don't like water, but if you think about where most of their food comes from, having cats connected to water makes sense. They are also sleek and graceful creatures that move as if they are in liquid motion. If you have a cat, put their favorite toys in the West or put a kitty condo there. If you grow catnip grass for your cat in this area, it will not only keep your cat healthy, but you as well. For many of us, cats in particular and household animals in general are not just pets. They are members of our families. By keeping them healthy, they keep us healthy. It's a proven medical fact that pets lower blood pressure and help relieve stress.

MUSICAL INSTRUMENTS. Any resonant metal musical instrument is also appropriately kept in the West. A singing bowl would be right at home here. If you are a belly dancer (or even if you are not) finger cymbals kept here will feel healthy every time you put them on. My husband tells a wonderful story about camping out at a lake one time. Someone had brought along a crystal singing bowl and played it late one night on the shore. The sound resonating across the water and back raised the hair, and not so incidentally the energy, of everyone present. That bowl was at home next to the water and the playfulness of its sound affected the entire group.

AGE. West is also the direction of maturity. Mother/Father-hood is strongest in the West. It is the time in our lives when our families are established and we are living life at its fullest. Family portraits hung in the West emphasize this attribute.

HOLIDAYS.   Ah, September. Golden air surrounds us as the leaves of the mighty oak and the apple trees reach their full ripeness. Days are still warm, but the nights begin to cool, ripening fruits on the vine, and bringing relief from the heat of summer. Days are shortening and preparations are being made for the coming winter. But it isn't here yet. The season is fall and Mabon is the holiday. We now enjoy the second harvest of our labors—fruits and nuts, squash and beans. Although our American calendar says that Thanksgiving is another two months away, for us Witches, it is at this time. We have tilled the soil, sown it, and now this is when we benefit from all that hard work. Cornucopias and harvest scenes belong in this area of your house.

TIME OF DAY/MOON CYCLE.   Days shorten and dusk seems to last forever in the fall. It is the time of day when, it is said, that it is easiest to enter the realm of Faery. We stand at the gates of the otherworld at dusk and we must remember to bring the spiritual realm into our lives in order to be healthy in all ways. The moon is waning as is the year and our busy summer lives are but a pleasant memory.

COLOR.   Water represents the emotions in our lives so having it flow clear and true helps keep our emotional balance on an even keel. The deep blue indigo of the ocean rules over our third eye reminding us to look beyond the mere physical when considering health and family. Body, mind, and soul joined together are essential to well-being.

STAR RUNES.   The following Star Runes should be viewed in the color indigo either by copying them onto indigo paper or by tracing the actual symbol in indigo.

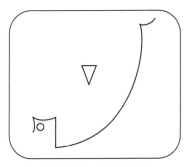

Figure 21. Third Eye, Clarity

The third eye increases our ability to see beyond the physical and into the spiritual. Clarity of purpose opens our minds to true intellect. Opening the third eye, we see beyond the limitations of the body and see past the masks of our family members. We also see beyond our own masks and embrace true health.

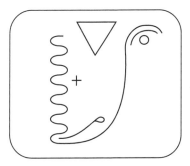

Figure 22. Mind, Reasoning, Attunement

The full power of the mind is beyond human comprehension. A few scratch the surface of our reasoning abilities, but attunement is the key to the full use of our minds. Only when we transcend our physical limitations can health truly be achieved.

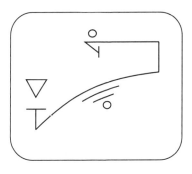

Figure 23. Navigation, Direction, Future Map, Guidance, "Coming Home"

Without direction and maps, we quickly lose our way and wander without purpose. Navigation and guidance, be it from within or without, allows us to find our way home to the bosom of our families.

NUMBER. Without our health, everything else in our lives becomes a struggle, so the number one is the number of Health and Family. This seems like a strange number for an area that rules family as well as health until you consider that we must care for ourselves *first* if we expect to be able to care for others. Having only one fountain flowing or only one fish in a bowl, you reinforce the power of this area.

TAROT. If you have a collection of tea cups or if you like to display your wine glasses, show them off in the West. The Tarot suit of this area is Cups and all things reminiscent of Chalices are appropriate here.

Drink from the waters of the Goddess for health and family.

Consecration Ritual

Once you have chosen the enhancements for your Health and Family Bagua area, you will want to perform the following ritual to consecrate those items. This ritual is best done at dusk during a Waning Moon, since that is the time of day and moon cycle associated with the West.

YOU WILL NEED:
Your athame
The bowl of water from your main altar
A dark blue candle.

Choose a Goddess and God associated with Water, oceans, rivers, West, harvest, or autumn. I am presenting this ritual with Boann and Bran, but please feel free to change these to deities you work well with.

Prepare yourself as you would for any magickal working, and prepare the space according to your traditions.

Facing due West, invoke the Goddess and God asking them to be with you as you consecrate these sacred items.

Boann, Goddess of the mighty river.
Be with me to bless and consecrate these items so that they may keep this dwelling alive with the power of still and flowing waters.

So Mote It Be!

Bran the Blessed, God of the Waning Year.
Be with me to bless and consecrate these items so that they may keep this dwelling alive with the power of still and flowing waters.

So Mote It Be!

Light the dark blue candle. Call the element of Water to be present in the candle and the water bowl as you touch your athame to each in turn, and say:

Guardians of the West,
Powers of Water,
Be with me to bless and consecrate these items so that they may keep this dwelling alive with the power of still and flowing waters.

The light of your purity, health, and love permeates this
        _____ [touch athame to chosen enhancements].
Burn bright in my home for now and evermore.

Sprinkle water on the enhancements, and say:

I bless and consecrate these items with the Water of the West.
May Health and Family reign within my home.
So Mote It Be!

Thank you Guardians of the West,
Powers of Water.
Go in Peace

Thank you Boann,
Go in Peace.

Thank you Bran,
Go in Peace.

It is done!

Let the candle burn until it goes out on its own. Your Bagua area of Health and Family is now set.
The ritual is ended.

Magickal Workings

Now that the Health and Family area of your home is consecrated, you may wish to perform certain rituals or place specific items in this area that relate to health and family. You can choose something from the list below, or add your own suggestions in the space provided.

Rituals for:	*Items:*
Purification	Photos of long lost friends that
Friendship	you wish to return
Psychic awareness	Family games
Sleep	Picnic basket
Emotional stability	
Health	

My Ideas:

South—Love and Marriage

Everyone loves sitting in front of a roaring fire. The heat from the flames spreads throughout your entire body bringing with it a feeling of peace and contentment. The flames leap from one area to another, dancing along the edges of the wood as they seem to dance in the air around you. Sparks escape up the chimney or flash an uncaught area of wood. It slowly smolders until it, too, bursts into flame. The coals burn red-hot keeping the fire from going out completely. Wiccan Feng Shui is the screen and fireplace that keeps the fire where it belongs. It is also the poker that stokes up the coals and brings those flames alive again and again.

Due South is the Bagua area of Love and Marriage. In its conventional definition, love and marriage is, well . . . love and marriage. Going beyond the obvious, we can love *things* as well as people. Chocolate has to be one of the great loves of many of my friends, myself included. A business partnership can be seen as a marriage. Marrying thought and action is a common phrase. Anytime we come together to integrate ideas or feelings, that's a marriage. Making a promise to be together no matter what is a marriage, even if no formal or legal vows have been taken.

I think it's pretty obvious by now that the element that belongs in the South is Fire, so the most common enhancement in the southern area of your home is a fireplace. If you're lucky enough to have a fireplace in its place of honor, you need do nothing else to enhance this area. Make sure that you clean out the fireplace every spring and dispose of the ashes either by scattering them in your garden or in a natural area. Plants love ash and you are returning what was once Earth, back to it! In the warmer months keep at least one candle on the hearth or in the fireplace itself. Nowadays there are wonderful hearth candelabras that are made for this purpose. Don't put a plant in your empty fireplace. A plant will smother the Fire in your life the same way that Earth smothers a fire.

If you don't have a fireplace in the South or if your fireplace is located in a different direction, you can use other enhancements in this area. Two red candles are best since red is the color associated with this area with the number two representing partnerships. Make sure the candles are the same size and type if you are married or you may find one partner trying to dominate the relationship. Candle sconces are a perfect way to enhance this area as well as being an elegant addition to your home.

Since this is the area of Love and Marriage, it is the perfect place to hang a wedding photo or store a wedding album.

AGE.   The South is also about all things adult. Childhood is gone and it is time to take responsibility for our actions. I know what you are thinking: "But I don't want to grow up!" Who said anything about growing up? I'm one of the biggest kids I know! When you reach the South you know that you have survived adolescence. We leave home and begin to establish ourselves in the outside world. As teenagers, we are so anxious to be adults, yet once we get to that stage, we bemoan our fate. Nonsense! We are in the prime of our lives. Now is the time when we truly begin to understand ourselves without the pressures of school and parents. This is the time when everything is in full bloom. The summer of our lives.

METALS.   Any work of art that depicts love is best here especially if it has gold or brass highlights, as these are the metals that belong in the South.

CRYSTALS.   Red garnet, rose quartz, smoky quartz, and black obsidian can be placed here as less obvious enhancements. For more energy in your partnerships use red garnet. Rose quartz can help you here if you are recovering from a broken heart or if you need to love *yourself* more. When we love ourselves we are more fully capable of loving others.

When trying to bring love into your life, smoky quartz helps by dispersing any psychic blocks you may have toward love. It also relieves jealousies and misunderstandings.

If you have a black obsidian orb, place it on a brass stand underneath a photo of you and your love, if the two of you have been angry at each other. Black obsidian helps release anger. Or, you can place two wall sconces on either side of the photo and now you have a shrine to love!

ANIMALS.   Do you have an affinity for desert creatures? Make their homes here. Snakes, lizards, and iguanas will all feel at home in the southern part of your house. Snakes especially! Snakes have long been associated with sexual energy. Their very shapes are phallic in nature and the way in which they wind around each other when mating is sensual and all-encompassing. The regenerative ability of snakes makes itself known when they shed their skins. In a sense, we do the same when we enter into a marriage; we intertwine and cast off our old lives, forming a new one with our partner. If a snake is out of the question in your home, even a representation of one, anything that spirals or has a spiral in it will also enhance this area.

MUSICAL INSTRUMENTS.   Have a guitar? Store it in the South when you're not using it. Singing around the campfire has its place in your home as well. Any instrument with strings is an instrument of Fire, including violin, bass, and cello.

HOLIDAYS.   Summer is the season of the South. Warmth and fun. Summer Solstice, the time of the great marriage when we establish ourselves as our own family. Aha! Makes sense, doesn't it? Litha is the holiday that belongs in the South. Passion and joy abound. Our days are at their strongest and longest. Enjoy this time: Drum, dance, make love; Celebrate the heights of ecstasy. Anything that reminds you of summer is a wonderful addition to your southern altar; a ceramic sun, sunflower seeds, or a golden mask.

TIME OF DAY/MOON CYCLE.   Midday seems to last forever at Summer Solstice. We have our picnics at noon and that time of day is the most joyful of all in the summer. Everything is at its fullest in the South, even the moon. Once the sun has set, the full moon continues Her dance bringing a brightness like day to the landscape around us.

COLOR.   The vibrant color of Fire is red. Red is the color of our most basic emotions. It is at the root of our life—inspiration, courage, abundant energy, and sex are all associated with the color red. In the Orient, brides wear red wedding gowns for it is considered to be a color of joy. In this country, our most romantic holiday, Valentine's Day, is full of red hearts and plush red teddy bears. If you decide to enhance this area with a wedding photo, put it in a red frame or mat. Red is also the color of blood and when we are "in love," it pumps faster through our veins. Heat up this area by using lots of red.

STAR RUNES.   The Star Runes opposite should be viewed in the color red either by copying them onto red paper or by tracing the actual symbol in red.

NUMBER.   The number two is the number for this area representing partnership and marriage. There is strength in numbers and the number two is a number of safety as well. I do believe

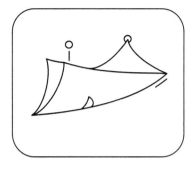

Figure 24. Travel, Direction, Transportation

Movement in our daily lives brings a sense of purpose to everyday activities, but we must have a direction to travel before we can progress toward the realization that we are not static beings, even if we only travel within ourselves. When we have love in our lives, our direction changes and we transport ourselves into new and exciting places. If you are wavering over a partnership, focus on the Star Rune to help in the decision-making process.

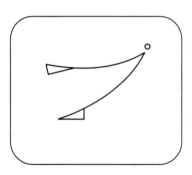

Figure 25. Courage, Bravery

Maintaining the courage of our convictions in the midst of others with the same beliefs is easy, but being aggressive and asserting our beliefs when we are alone in them makes us truly brave. This Star Rune helps us to keep our individuality even while joined with another.

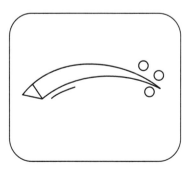

Figure 26. Fatherhood, God Energy, Relationships with Men, Sexual Energy

The relationships with men in our lives bring us a deeper understanding of the phrase "just do it." God energy is a powerful motivator inspiring us to reach out and acquire what we need in our lives, and to do so without hesitation.

that it is possible to be in love with more than one person at a time and to have more than one partner in business. The number two takes nothing away from that energy. On the contrary, the power of two reinforces the strength of love and marriage regardless of the number of people involved.

TAROT.   Swords is the Tarot suit for South, but I don't recommend displaying your ritual sword here, because South is the area of Love and Marriage and by displaying sharp instruments and weapons here, you may inadvertently cause conflicts in your close relationships. Keep that suit in mind, however, when performing rituals in this area. You wouldn't think that Swords, typically the suit representing business, belongs in Love and Marriage, but business partnerships are most definitely similar to marriages. If you love your work, then all areas of your life flow easier.

The Fire of your spiritual life is brightest in the South, but be careful, spiritual understanding can be as sharp as the blades of your sword. Tread carefully so you do not hurt yourself or others. It takes practice to wield that sword. Take it slow.

Consecration Ritual

Once you have chosen the enhancements for your Love and Marriage Bagua area, you will want to perform the following ritual to consecrate those items. This ritual is best done at noon during a Full Moon, since that is the time of day and moon cycle associated with South.

YOU WILL NEED:
Your athame
The candle from your main altar
An additional red candle

Choose a Goddess and God associated with Fire, snakes, love, the Sun, South, or summer. I am presenting this ritual with Brigid and Sithehenn, but please feel free to change these to deities you work well with.

Prepare yourself as you would for any magickal working, and prepare the space according to your traditions.

Facing due South, invoke the Goddess and God, asking them to be with you as you consecrate these sacred items.

Brigid, Goddess of Fire, inspiration, and smithcraft.
Be with me to bless and consecrate these items so that they
     may keep this dwelling alive with the power of Fire and
     the warmth of the Summer sun.

So Mote It Be!

Sithehenn, God of Fire and consecration.
Be with me to bless and consecrate these items so that they
     may keep this dwelling alive with the power of Fire and
     the warmth of the Summer sun.

So Mote It Be!

Light both candles. Call the element of Fire to be present in the candles as you touch your athame to each in turn, and say:

Guardians of the South,
Powers of Fire,
Be with me to bless and consecrate these items so that they
     may keep this dwelling alive with the power of Fire and
     the warmth of the Summer sun.

The light of your inspiration, courage, and love permeates
     this _____ [touch athame to chosen enhancements].
Burn bright in my home for now and evermore.

Pass the enhancements through the flames of the red candles, and say:

I bless and consecrate these items with the Fire of the South.
May Love and Marriage reign within my home.

So Mote It Be!

Thank you Guardians of the South,
Powers of Fire.
Go in Peace.

Thank you Brigid,
Go in Peace.

Thank you Sithehenn,
Go in Peace.

It is done!

Let the red candle burn until it goes out on its own. Your Bagua area of Love and Marriage is now set.
The ritual is ended.

Magickal Workings

Now that the Love and Marriage area of your home is consecrated, you may wish to perform certain rituals or place specific items in this area that relate to Love and Marriage. You can use something from the list below, or add some of your own ideas in the space provided.

Rituals for:
Love
Marriage
Partnership
Purification
Courage
Spiritual Understanding
Energy
Strength
Sex
Inspiration
Banishing negativity
Creation through destruction

Items:
Wedding photos
Love letters
Workout equipment
Poetry books

My Ideas:

East—Creativity and Children

There is something special about opening all the windows in your house on a fresh spring day. The first warm breeze of the season blows gently through your house. As it meanders through open windows and doors, the dust and darkness of winter is carried away, leaving only freshness behind. That fresh wind stirs up feelings of creation and you long to start that new home improvement project or finally get around to putting all those photos in albums. Looking outside, you notice the greening of the world and take delight in watching the young rabbits play among the new shoots of plants and budding leaves of the trees. Wiccan Feng Shui throws open those windows and encourages the winds of creation and creativity into your house.

Due East is the Bagua area of Creativity and Children. There are so many ways in life to be creative. You can be creative in your job no matter what it is. An accountant can be creative with numbers. A receptionist can be creative in the inflections in her voice as she answers the phone. Creativity at home involves meal planning, furniture arrangement, and gardening. And don't forget children! Children are the highest expression of creativity—the creation of a whole person!

Since Air is difficult to see, creativity can be difficult to grasp, so we want to find a way to capture creativity and bring it into our lives, or at least acknowledge its presence. A dream catcher is a beautiful way to enhance this Bagua area for it allows the wind to pass through it, but it grabs something in the process. Along these same lines is using a net of some sort. I display a net in the eastern part of my office that was used during one of my moon rituals. It reminds me of how elusive and yet, at the same time, how easily caught creativity can be. If you use a net, resist the temptation to fill it with fish! Fish are associated with Water not Air.

In Chapter 1 I mentioned the use of wind chimes to move Chi into areas that are stagnant. They are also appropriate in this Bagua area. Wind chimes are something that acknowledges the presence of Air by making joyful music.

Since we want creativity to flourish in our lives, a plant is useful here. Fern is good for protection, luck and riches, and lavender is good for longevity, happiness, and peace. A wax plant can be used for protection and to give spells some extra power. These are all excellent plant choices for this area.

On one of my more creative days I went to the local craft store and concocted a piece of "wall art" for this Bagua area. My husband couldn't believe it when he got home. I had covered one whole wall in our dining room with cloth butterflies! Since

I had no windows on my eastern wall, I bought a small mirror that looked like a windowpane and made a yellow lace curtain for it. I pinned it up on one side to make it look like a breeze had caught it and blown it open. I then proceeded to pin butterflies to the window, the curtain, and all the way up the wall. I also placed a silk ficus tree in front of the window with a butterfly on one of the leaves. The tree has a string of gold holiday lights on it that really adds drama to the whole scene at night. It was simple, inexpensive, fun, and fit the space perfectly. I get lots of compliments on it from guests. One of the darkest rooms in the house was transformed into one of the brightest!

Have fun with this space. That is really what creativity is all about. You don't have to be an interior designer to create spaces that speak to you.

METALS. Tin, copper, and aluminum are the metals common to the East, so you might want to get an aluminum window box and fill it with dried yellow flowers or if you have a piece of furniture with a punched tin facing, you could dedicate it to East. Copper pots hung in the eastern part of your kitchen inspire creative cooking.

AGE. Photos of your children or grandchildren are also good here, especially if the photo shows them sitting in a field of spring flowers, or flying a kite! If you have a kite, this would be a good place to display it. Anything that reminds you of childhood would be great here. A favorite toy, your baby blanket, an old lunchbox. A bookshelf filled with children's stories could adorn the wall. If you have children, this area is the best place for their toy box, but don't make that your official enhancement for toys move around too much and your enhancement needs to be something permanent.

CRYSTALS.   Citrine and turquoise are at home in the East. Citrine allows you to express your creativity in joyful and unique ways. It increases your powers of concentration and helps you to feel good about yourself and life in general. When we think of turquoise, most of us think of Native Americans. Silver and turquoise jewelry is very popular in states like New Mexico and Arizona where the population of Native Americans is very large. They have a lot on the ball and their belief systems are not that dissimilar from ours. Turquoise brings us attunement with Spirit. It is a peaceful stone that opens us to the beauty and harmony that surrounds us and, once in that state, our creativity can flow unimpeded.

ANIMALS.   A bird would be especially pleased to make his home in this part of your house. So would a pet tarantula, but it would probably be a good idea if they were in separate cages. If you don't have a bird or a spider, try buying an old birdcage, paint it yellow and use it to display something special or leave it as a display in and of itself. An old-fashioned wooden birdhouse, painted whimsically, would look great in this area.

Where does creativity come from? Good question, and one without a definitive answer. We are inspired by such a disparate set of circumstances in our lives that it is difficult to pin down creativity to something specific. Rabbits know. Have you ever seen a rabbit that was not creating other rabbits? They don't think about inspiration, they just follow their instincts. Intuition and fertility accompany the rabbit through spring. We can learn a lot about creativity from the rabbit, as well as the goose. The goose has a strong attachment to family and according to Druid lore represents parenthood. The goose provides security so your creative power can flourish. A goose-down comforter would be appropriate if your bed is in the East.

Do you have a collection of feathers sitting in a drawer somewhere? Get them out, dust them off, and display them in a hanging basket on your wall or create your own "wall art" with them. Keep curtains soft and flowing in this area.

MUSICAL INSTRUMENTS.   Play the flute or a panpipe? Even if you don't play, you can get one of these instruments for your own personal enhancement. It's better, of course, if they are used occasionally, but if not, they can still be art. Any wind instrument is appropriate here, including horns and reeds.

HOLIDAYS.   Ah, spring. The first warm breezes after the cold winter inspire us to get up, get out, and get moving. Open those windows and let those warm currents blow the dust away. It clears our houses and clears our minds. It's fresh and full of promise. Egg-shaped candies, pictures of bunnies, and seedlings bursting forth are all images of Ostara, the Spring Equinox. I have marble eggs that I keep in a basket this time of year and they have an honored place in my Bagua area of Creativity and Children.

TIME OF DAY/MOON CYCLE.   Spring is the awakening of the Earth and the dawn of a new growing season. To greet the dawn on the morning of the Spring Equinox will bring you visions of the coming year. My computer monitor sits on the East side of my desk and displays a sunrise photo that I took in the mountains of New Mexico several years ago. This inspires me to always start fresh every time I turn on my computer. The waxing of the moon reminds us that everything will grow stronger as we proceed through the year.

COLOR.   Sunshine yellow clears the cobwebs from our minds and opens our souls to the creative impulse. Have you ever noticed that if a couple chooses not to know the sex of their unborn child that they typically decorate the nursery with yellow? Intuitively they know that yellow belongs in this space. Yellow is the color of our solar plexus, the power center of our bodies. Make creativity the power center of your life!

STAR RUNES.   The following Star Runes should be viewed in the color yellow either by copying them onto yellow paper or by tracing the actual symbol in yellow.

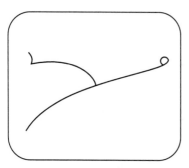

Figure 27. Trust, Openness

In opening ourselves to the power inherent in the universe, we trust ourselves to make the right decisions in life. In trusting others, we learn the most important lesson—both from loyalty and from betrayal—that we must remain open. Display this Star Rune if you are having trouble trusting your creativity.

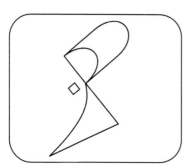

Figure 28. Power, Perpetual Motion

One of the great truths of the universe is the saying (and I'm paraphrasing here): "Objects at rest or in motion tend to stay that way until acted upon by an outside force." That outside force doesn't have to be physical. We often need to ask for a push to get us going, whether from a spirit guide or from our own higher selves. And once we have motion, it becomes perpetual, constantly renewing our power. Start that creativity flowing and it will extend itself into all areas of life.

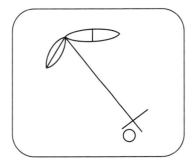

Figure 29. Growth, Expansion
The seed lies dormant waiting for the earth to warm before it can grow. Roots spring forth, hidden from the world, prior to the expansion that will break through the ground and bring us ever closer to the light of truth. Nurture creativity and it will always grow.

NUMBER. When a child is born into a family, two becomes three, so three is the number for Creativity and Children. Dreams and imagination abound with the number three. Remember those cloth butterflies I mentioned? There are nine of them on my wall, because nine is a multiple of three. Groupings of three are highly effective in this area.

TAROT. The great trees bend in the wind, so the Tarot suit for Air is Wands. Creativity is all about tapping into Spirit and letting it blow through our lives. Sometimes that creative urge is so strong that we feel as if we can fly. And we do! At least in our minds. Remembering that creativity exists within us and in everything that we do is the key to that flight. If you have a walking staff or wand, keep it here in its place of honor.

Wands represent the mental aspect of ourselves. Our minds are as clear as our houses after they have been opened up to the wind. Throw open your mental doors every once in a while and you will find your creativity soaring.

Consecration Ritual

Once you have chosen the enhancements for your Creativity and Children Bagua area, you will want to perform the following ritual to consecrate those items. This ritual is best done at dawn during a Waxing Moon since that is the time of day and moon cycle associated with East.

YOU WILL NEED:
Your athame
The incense from your main altar
A yellow candle

Choose a Goddess and God associated with the Air, birds, East, or spring. I will be presenting this ritual with Kore and Amergin, but please feel free to change these to deities you work well with.

Prepare yourself as you would for any magickal working and prepare the space according to your traditions.

Facing due East, invoke the Goddess and God asking them to be with you as you consecrate these sacred items.

Kore, Goddess of the breezes of Springtime.
Be with me to bless and consecrate these items so that they
*   may keep this dwelling alive with the power of freshness*
*   and new beginnings.*

So Mote It Be!

Amergin, God of Words and creativity.
Be with me to bless and consecrate these items so that they
*   may keep this dwelling alive with the power of freshness*
*   and new beginnings.*

So Mote It Be!

Light the yellow candle. Call the element of Air to be present in the candle and the incense as you touch your athame to each in turn, and say:

Guardians of the East,
Powers of Air,
Be with me to bless and consecrate these items so that they
may keep this dwelling alive with the power of freshness
and new beginnings.

The light of your creation, freshness, and clarity permeates
this _____ [touch athame to chosen enhancements].
Burn bright in my home for now and evermore.

Saturate the enhancements with the smoke from the incense, and say:

I bless and consecrate these items with the Power of Air.
May Creativity and Children reign within my home.

So Mote It Be!

Thank you Guardians of the East,

Powers of Air.
Go in Peace.

Thank you Kore,
Go in Peace.

Thank you Amergin,
Go in Peace.

It is done!

Let the yellow candle burn until it goes out on its own. Your Bagua area of Creativity and Children is now set.
The ritual is ended.

Magickal Workings

Now that the Creativity and Children area of your home is consecrated, you may wish to perform certain rituals or place specific items in this area that relate to creativity and children. You can use some of the suggestions from the list below or add some of your own in the space provided.

Rituals for:	*Items:*
Creativity	Books
Freedom	Telephone
Knowledge	Maps
Recovering lost items	Toys
Mental clarity	Crayons
Conception	Coloring books
New Beginnings	Games

My ideas:

The Cross Quarters

There is no difference in importance between the Quarters and the Cross-Quarters when it comes to the Bagua areas. The difference lies in the elements and enhancements. Whereas the Quarters are specifically related to certain elements, the Cross-Quarters share the attributes of the elements on both sides of it. Not only does it share the elements, but it also shares the enhancements. Each Bagua area has enhancements specific to it, which I will be discussing in this section. However, you can also use enhancements from either element bracketing a specific area. For example: for the Career area in the NorthWest, you can add a plant from Earth or a piece of Lapis from Water or both. Consecrate the plant when you consecrate all northern pieces and then simply move it to the NorthWest. Then, include it in the consecration of the enhancements for the NorthWest. A double consecration! How much more powerful can you get?

The Cross-Quarters represent the outside forces that affect our internal lives. These are the public areas of our lives and as such require other people to make them work.

NorthWest—Career

Imagine sitting on the beach. An occasional wave reaches up to gently tug at you enticing you to play in its foamy waters. But you're busy. You're building. You're being productive. And the sandcastle is shaping up! Occasionally, you walk to the sea to scoop up some water, bringing it back to help shape your walls or to build turrets of wet sand. Then, you scoop dry sand in your hands to give your castle a light dusting and soften the lines. Now it is more pleasing to the eye. Your castle is finished and, proud of your accomplishments, you plunge into the water for a refreshing swim and to cleanse yourself of the grubbiness of the sand. Walking up the beach, you sit in the twilight by a warm fire, feeling the salty breeze slowly drying your hair and watch the sea carry away your creation. But that's okay. There is plenty of sand and water and, after all, as Scarlett O'Hara said, "Tomorrow *is* another day." Wiccan Feng Shui helps you shape your castle and constantly reminds you that, even if your creation gets washed away, you can build it again tomorrow and if you want it to stay a little longer, experience tells you to build it a little farther up the beach.

Between Wealth and Prosperity and Health and Family lies Career; a perfect reminder that we must balance our career between these two aspects of our lives. When one dominates the other we lose sight of why we have a career in the first place, to support our families, but also to support ourselves. There is no fudging on this definition. Your career is your career is your career. An old saying goes, that if you can get paid for doing something you truly love then you'll never work another day in your life. We must redefine work in our lives and appreciate our jobs for what they do—namely feed our families and provide us with material comfort—even if we feel stifled or are unhappy. Work is a four-letter word. But a career enhances our lives, just as the following enhancements will improve, or maintain, our careers.

The following is a good daily ritual that will help you get out of "job" mode and into "family" mode when you get home from work.

Ritual

Walk in the door and immediately proceed to the Career Bagua area of your home. Take a few minutes to review the day's events and problems or update your planner. Once finished, take a deep breath and say:

"Work is done for the day. Now is family time [or
relationship time, or creativity time]."

Walk purposefully toward the Bagua area of your choice and take a few minutes to focus on the enhancement in that area. State either aloud or silently the way you intend to spend the evening. This can be as general as "time with family" or as specific as, "clean out my sock drawer." You will be amazed at how much extra time you will have for things in your life other than work and how focused you will be on those things. This is a much better way to step out of career mode than to try "leaving it at the office."

The ritual is ended.

Since the Career Bagua area is sandwiched between Earth and Water, enhancements from either of these elements is appropriate here, just make sure you don't end up with a muddy mess. The best enhancement for this area is anything having to do with your career, but be careful not to overdo it. Keep this enhancement simple or you will find your career issues becoming more complex.

The Career Bagua area in my house is in the master bedroom, so I have chosen not to have anything to do with work in this area. Instead, I painted my ceiling a light blue with puffy white clouds. This is incredibly relaxing as I lie in bed because it doesn't remind me directly of work, yet it enhances this area in my home. My home office is, in reality, my career center although it is located in my Wealth and Prosperity Bagua area. After a day spent in my office, I take the time to lie on my bed and stare at the ceiling which pulls me out of work and allows me to leave the day's events "at the office." If you work at home, place your desk in the Career area of your home office. Store your briefcase or daily planner here when you get home.

There are several other ways to enhance this area that are not reminiscent of work directly.

CRYSTALS.   A large clear quartz cluster is a great enhancement for the area because it shows all the different facets that a career entails. Sodalite and azurite are also great in this area. Sodalite grounds you in your career while allowing you to reach toward the spiritual. Azurite keeps communications clear and helps you express difficult ideas or concepts to others. Your boss will be impressed!

ANIMALS.   An ant farm represents teamwork and a common sense of purpose. Ever heard the expressions "he works like a dog" or "she's a real workhorse"? A ceramic dog or horse would fit perfectly into this space. A ram is also an excellent choice to represent career as it is patient and stable. Even on the pinnacle of a mountain, the ram will never forget that he must keep his footing sure or he will lose his position.

A frog reminds us to look beyond appearance and see what is really there. This concept is most important in your career. You never know if that frog you have to kiss during a big project could turn out to be a prince. The frog also shares one of his homes with shellfish. Lobsters and crabs remind us of the politics in our workplaces. We must keep a tough outer shell in order to succeed and sometimes a sideways scuttle is the best way to avoid trouble.

MUSICAL INSTRUMENTS.   Musical instruments tend to denote relaxation and free time. So, unless you're a professional musician, store your musical instruments elsewhere.

HOLIDAYS.   "Gathering to turn the wheel" is an expression commonly used to define the celebration of Samhain. Appropriate to Career, don't you think? Working in harmony to make sure projects go smoothly. You may think that Samhain is an odd holiday to represent Career, but it really makes sense if you think about it. No matter what your career, I guarantee that it consists of beginnings and endings. Having to finish one project before starting another, be it a proposal, a piece of equipment, or a song. My career is full of beginnings and endings. Each chapter in a section, each section in a book, each book in a series, and so on. So when you think of career, think of Samhain and a whole new set of enhancements will present themselves. Masks on the wall and ghost stories on the bookshelf might get you started in this vein. Have fun and don't be scared to express yourself in unusual ways.

COLOR.   The light blue of a clear daytime sky is the color for career. No matter how stormy it may get, the sky will always clear as long as we keep our communications flowing and unfettered by storm clouds. Light blue is the color of communication, which is centered on our throats. When you're feeling nervous about a conversation, try imagining a stream of blue from your throat to whomever you are talking to. This promotes understanding and keeps thoughts pure and flowing freely, reminding us to remain focused on the sky and not on the clouds.

STAR RUNES.   The following Star Runes should be viewed in the color light blue either by copying them onto light blue paper or by tracing the actual symbol in light blue.

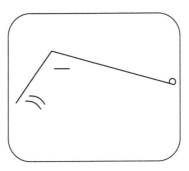

Figure 30. Dreams, Subconscious Mind

"To sleep. Perchance, to dream." Shakespeare said it best. Dreams are our subconscious minds communicating with us. To pay special attention to our dreams and the symbolism in our lives brings us closer to the core of our being. We must dream it before we can be it, and this is especially true in our careers.

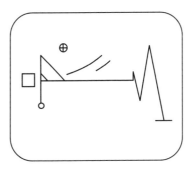

Figure 31. Multisource Information

Information from only one source always leaves us with a skewed perspective. Wading through and disseminating information from many different sources brings us closer to truth and understanding. If you are feeling overwhelmed with too many projects at work, focus on this Star Rune to help you break down massive amounts of information.

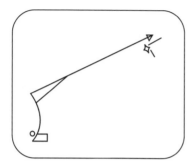

Figure 32. Service to Others, Speaking Out, Justice

True justice lies not in others or in a governmental system. True justice lies in speaking out our truths, whatever they may be, without attachment to the final outcome. In this way, we truly serve others and ourselves. For courage in speaking your mind to others at work, use this Star Rune as a focus.

NUMBER.   The number eight represents money and power in our lives, two very important aspects of our careers. The number eight can also be seen as a second foundation in our lives, strengthening the number four (Wealth and Prosperity) by reinforcing it.

TAROT.   I meditated long and hard on the Tarot trump for this area and what was finally revealed was the Devil. For those of you who are familiar with the Tarot, this makes a strange kind of sense. For those of you who are not, let me explain. The Devil is not an evil character to most Witches, because he is a character that most of us do not relate to. He doesn't exist in our religion. In the Tarot, however, he represents that which can become a master. We tend to voluntarily chain ourselves to our jobs, then find it difficult to break free when we need to. This card is a reminder to not become a workaholic. Work is an important part of our lives, no doubt, but we must remember that it is only a *part* of our lives and not the whole. Lecture over.

Consecration Ritual

Once you have chosen the enhancements for your Career Bagua area, you will want to perform the following ritual to consecrate those items. This ritual is best done in between dusk and midnight, and between a Waning and Dark Moon since that is the time of day and moon cycle associated with NorthWest.

YOU WILL NEED:
Your athame
The saucer of salt and the bowl of water off your
    main altar
A light blue candle

Choose a Goddess and God most closely associated with the Samhain, Earth, Water or both, or with the type of work you do. I will be presenting this ritual with Gonlod and Mercury, but please feel free to change these to deities you work well with.

Prepare yourself as you would for any magickal working and prepare the space according to your traditions.

Facing NorthWest, invoke the Goddess and God asking them to be with you as you consecrate these sacred items.

Gonlod, Goddess of Poetry, Holder of the Cauldron of
*   Inspiration.*
Be with me to bless and consecrate these items so that they
*   may keep this dwelling alive with the power of my*
*   vocation.*

So Mote It Be!

Mercury, God of Communication, Great Messenger.
Be with me to bless and consecrate these items so that they
*   may keep this dwelling alive with the power of my vocation.*

So Mote It Be!

Light the light blue candle. Call the elements of the North to be present in the candle and the salt while you touch your athame to each in turn, and say:

Guardians of the North,
Powers of Earth,
Be with me to bless and consecrate these items so that they
    may keep this dwelling alive with the power of my
    vocation.

The light of your strength, stability, fertility, and growth
    permeates this _____ [touch athame to chosen
    enhancements].
Burn bright in my home for now and evermore.

Sprinkle salt on the enhancements.

I bless and consecrate these items with the salt of the Earth.
May my Career be nurtured.

So Mote It Be!

Call the element of the West to be present in the candle
and the water bowl as you touch your athame to each in
turn, and say:

Guardians of the West,
Powers of Water,
Be with me to bless and consecrate these items so that they
    may keep this dwelling alive with the power of my
    vocation.

The light of your purity, health, and love permeates this
    _____ [touch athame to chosen enhancements].
Burn bright in my home for now and evermore.

Sprinkle water on the enhancements.

I bless and consecrate these items with the Water of the West.

May my Career be nurtured.

So Mote It Be!

Thank you Guardians of the North,
Powers of Earth,
Go in Peace.

Thank you Guardians of the West,
Powers of Water.
Go in Peace.

Thank you Gonlod.
Go in Peace.

Thank you Mercury,
Go in Peace.

It is done!

Let the candle burn until it goes out on its own. Your Bagua area of Career is now set.

The ritual is ended.

Magickal Workings

Now that the Career area of your home is consecrated, you may wish to perform certain rituals or place specific items in this area that relate to career. You can choose something from the list below or add your own suggestions in the space provided.

Rituals for:	*Items:*
Job changes	Briefcase
Employment issues	Desk
Communication	Want ads
Grief (Samhain)	Day planner
Breaking addictions	Calendar
Endings	

My ideas:

SouthWest—Fame and Reputation

Imagine yourself sitting at the edge of a natural hot spring on a warm summer day. You look across the pool, but find your vision obscured by the steam rising from the water. The shapes on the other side are shifting and elusive, so you plunge into the water and move toward those figures. The hot water relaxes your muscles and the steam clears your head as the sun warms your soul. You see the shape in front of you clearly, but the one behind it is soft and undefined and you find it impossible to focus on more than one shape at a time. Finally, you give up and cease struggling. You feel relaxed and energetic, healthy and confident. Wiccan Feng Shui shows us that Fame and Reputation is not something to be sought, but something that happens gradually over the course of time. By focusing only on what is directly in front of us before floating on to the next thing, our reputation is earned. But in the meantime, here are some water wings and eucalyptus oil to help us along.

Between Health and Family and Love and Marriage lies Fame and Reputation. We bring new people into our lives, be they lovers or friends, through our reputation. Sometimes our reputation precedes us and people we have never met have already made up their minds about us. And if the reputation is a bad one, you may never meet that person, missing out on one of life's great experiences—interaction with new people. On the other hand, as a good reputation grows it can transform into fame. Fame is an elusive concept until you think about it as a simple extension of your reputation. You can be famous in your own circle of friends even if you never win that Academy Award you dreamed about as a kid.

Since we want our reputations to grow, a plant is a great enhancement for this area. A small fruit-bearing tree is appropriate here as well as most types of herbs. If you grow your own herbs, I suggest researching the herbs you grow to make sure they represent something you wish to be known for. While decorating this area keep in mind that this area, above any other, represents how the outside world perceives you.

Since the Fame and Reputation Bagua area is sandwiched between Water and Fire, enhancements from either one of these elements is appropriate here. In the right combination you'll end up with steam. A steamy reputation can be fun for a while and you can make it hotter by adding a little Fire or tone it down with more Water. Make sure this area is bright and clear. If it's dark, so will be your reputation. If it's disorganized, so will be your reputation. And so on. Choose carefully.

My husband and I had fun with this Bagua area in our house. Since we are both very active and love social situations, especially when we are in the middle of them, we put our name in lights. Literally. We bought rope lighting in purple from our local bargain store and put our initials on the wall in lights. It gets lots of comments and it's just plain fun. If this is a little too much for you, that's okay, I have more suggestions.

CRYSTALS.   An amethyst geode would be a beautiful focal point for this area, as would purple fluorite. Amethyst transmutes and deflects negative energy, so if someone is telling lies about you and trying to ruin your reputation, amethyst is your antidote. Incredibly complex structures exist within fluorite clusters reminding us that our reputation has many different facets. With fluorite as your enhancement, you can better grasp variety and enjoy the simple beauty of a complex structure.

ANIMALS.   A pet turtle would be very happy here because turtles are slow moving, but long living, and they are creatures often associated with royalty. If you would rather have a fast reputation, choose a cat as the symbol for this area. Cats are not only fast, but they have an incredible depth of patience and can sit for hours waiting for just the right moment to act. If they don't get exactly what they want, they realize that other opportunities will soon present themselves. A positive attitude, especially where your reputation is concerned, is important.

In order to earn a good reputation we must be diplomatic with others, friends as well as enemies. The cunning of the fox is of great help here. Sometimes we must let others know that they cannot speak ill of us without consequences. The scorpion within us lets people know that if they leave us alone nothing will happen to them, but if they go rooting around in the dark, watch out!

HOLIDAYS.   Lammas or Lughnassadh is the first harvest of the year—the harvest of grains—and the holiday associated with this Bagua area. Just as wheat reaches its fullness at Lammas, so we reach our fullness in the outside world through our fame and reputation. Our fame and reputation can transform those around us just as wheat is transformed into bread. Sometimes, that takes sacrifice. We may sacrifice some little piece of our own reputation in order to bolster another's, or give up personal fame for the glory of being a small part of a much larger project. Fame and reputation is the give and take of wheat and bread. Celebrate this sacrifice by placing a single wheat sheaf in your Fame and Reputation Bagua area as a reminder to look beyond the personal and think about the whole.

COLOR.   Purple, the color of royalty. What a great color for this area! Not too much though or you may find your reputation one of arrogance or snobbery. Keep your enhancements simple in this area and you'll find your reputation growing slowly by itself. Purple is the color that emanates from the crown of our heads. It is from this place that we act for the greater good. When we have no thought of own rewards, our reputation is earned.

STAR RUNES.   The following Star Runes should be viewed in the color purple either by copying them onto purple paper or by tracing the actual symbol in purple.

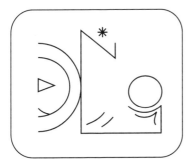

Figure 33. Self-Integration, Understanding the Complexities of the Human Condition

By understanding others, we better understand ourselves. In the most complex forms lie the simplest equations. Integrating these ideas within ourselves combines and joins us to each other and, in essence, melds us with the universe as a whole. This is an excellent Star Rune to focus upon if you do a lot of volunteer work.

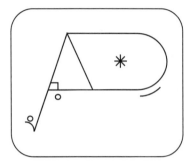

Figure 34. Teaching, Bringing Others to a Spiritual Home

The best teachers bring others to a spiritual home. It matters less what home that is than that the students find a way that completes them as individuals. Setting another's feet upon a path is a noble and rewarding vocation. We are all teachers in our own way, even if we never see the fruits of our labors. Each path is complete within itself.

Figure 35. Home, Contentment, Spiritual Pathways

At last we find through all our journeys outward that true contentment lies at home. Our spiritual pathways lead us to a better understanding of ourselves and the people around us. Our home is within us when we are content with ourselves.

NUMBER.   The number seven, oh, that lucky number seven! That magical, mystical number seven! Just like the dice game of craps, the number seven can cause you to either win or lose depending on when it is thrown. Keep it simple and quit while you are ahead if you want to garner a good reputation and become a famous player. Only in this game, it is about more than money; it is about your good name!

TAROT.   When we think of someone famous, we usually think of a "star." But in the Tarot, the Star is much more than Fame, it is recognizing the full potential inside of you. Whether that potential will actually make you a "star" or not is up to you.

But through your reputation and the realization of that potential, you can become a star in your own right.

See you at the Oscars!

Consecration Ritual

Once you have chosen the enhancements for your Fame and Reputation Bagua area, you will want to perform the following ritual to consecrate those items. This ritual is best done in the middle of the afternoon, in between a Full and Waning Moon since that is the time of day and moon cycle associated with SouthWest.

YOU WILL NEED:
Your athame
The bowl of water and red candle off your main altar
A purple candle.

Choose a Goddess and God most closely associated with Lammas, with Water, Fire, or both, or with how you wish to be perceived in the outside world. I will be presenting this ritual with Deborah and Lugh, but please feel free to change these to deities you work well with.

Prepare yourself as you would for any magickal working and prepare the space according to your traditions.

Facing SouthWest invoke the Goddess and God asking them to be with you as you consecrate these sacred items.

Deborah, Goddess of Justice, Great Poet.
Be with me to bless and consecrate these items so that they may keep this dwelling alive with the power of a strong and true reputation.

So Mote It Be!

Lugh, God of the Sun, Great Sacrifice.
Be with me to bless and consecrate these items so that they
*   may keep this dwelling alive with the power of a strong*
*   and true reputation.*

So Mote It Be!

Light the purple candle. Call the element of Water to be present in the purple candle and the water bowl as you touch your athame to each in turn, and say:

Guardians of the West,
Powers of Water,
Be with me to bless and consecrate these items so that they
*   may keep this dwelling alive with the power of a strong*
*   and true reputation.*

The light of your purity, health, and love permeates this
*   _____ [touch athame to chosen enhancements].*
Burn bright in my home for now and evermore.

Sprinkle water on the enhancements, and say:

I bless and consecrate these items with the Water of the
*   West.*
May my Fame and Reputation stay strong and true.

So Mote It Be!

Call the element of Fire to be present in both of the candles as you touch your athame to each in turn, and say:

Guardians of the South,
Powers of Fire,
Be with me to bless and consecrate these items so that they
*   may keep this dwelling alive with the power of Fire and*
*   the warmth of the Summer sun.*

*The light of your inspiration, courage, and love permeates
this _____ [touch athame to chosen*
enhancements].
Burn bright in my home for now and evermore.

Pass the enhancements through the flame of the red
candle, and say:

*I bless and consecrate these items with the Fire of the
South.*
May my Fame and Reputation stay strong and true.

So Mote It Be!

Thank you Guardians of the West,
Powers of Water.
Go in Peace.

Thank you Guardians of the South,
Powers of Fire.
Go in Peace.

Thank you Deborah,
Go in Peace.

Thank you Lugh,
Go in Peace.

It is done!

Let the purple candle burn until it goes out on its own.
Your Bagua area of Fame and Reputation is now set.
The ritual is ended.

Magickal Workings

Now that the Fame and Reputation area of your home is consecrated, you may wish to perform certain rituals or place specific items in this area that relate to fame and reputation. You can choose from the list below or add your own in the space provided.

Rituals for:
Recognition
Transformation
Sacrifice
Harvest
Cunning
Patience
Community

Items:
Anything you wish to be
  recognized for:
Arts & Crafts
Music
Cooking
Volunteerism

My ideas:

SouthEast—Helpful People and Travel

Ah, camping is wonderful. The great outdoors. Fresh Air. Early morning chill. It's time to stoke up the fire from the night before and start the day. After exposing the coals and laying on some kindling, you bend down and blow. A few sparks fall on the kindling and flare up, then go out. You try again, but to no avail. The camp is stirring and people want their coffee, but no matter how hard you try you can't get the kindling to start. You soon find yourself out of breath, a little light-headed and wishing for a bellows. You turn your back and prepare the coffeepot and upon turning around you find your camp mates have gathered and are all blowing on the embers. The fire flares and each member of the camp adds more wood and takes turns at stoking the fire. The coffee is soon ready and plans are made for the day. Wiccan Feng Shui makes you secure in the knowledge that you can walk away and do your own thing during the day and when you return in the evening, the fire will, once again, flare up with a little help from your friends.

Between Love and Marriage and Creativity and Children lies Helpful People and Travel. This is the most active Bagua area of the entire chart and most of those activities are carried on outside the home. We form temporary partnerships at work, bringing together creativity and a spirit of cooperation in order to complete projects, and then we travel on to the next project and possibly a whole new set of Helpful People. This is true in all outside activities and non-home-based hobbies—coming together, creating, and then traveling on. That travel can be as close as across the street or as far as another country or continent. We need people in order to travel; airline reservationists, taxi drivers, hotel clerks. So Helpful People and Travel is intricately interwoven with and carries influences from Love and Marriage and Creativity and Children.

Since Helpful People and Travel is located between Air and Fire, enhancements from either of these two elements is appropriate here. Since this area is the most active one in the Bagua map, the best enhancement is something that moves. A wonderful literal enhancement is a freestanding globe that turns. It's representative of travel to places both near and far. Spin it and dream of faraway places. The magick of the movement will bring those travel dreams into focus. The more you want to travel, the more travel-related items should be kept in this area of your house such as a road atlas or series of maps. If it's your dream to one day visit Ireland, buy a decorative map of Ireland, frame it and hang it on the wall.

CRYSTALS.   Carnelian and tiger's-eye are the stones that belong in this area. You can add any of these to a wind chime, embed them in an orange candle, or simply use one of the crystals alone as your enhancement.

Carnelian is a powerful stone that increases vitality and assertiveness. It can help you add humor to any situation involving other people, making it a perfect stone for this area. Courage and endurance are inherent in tiger's-eye and it helps break down obstacles you may find in your path. Tiger's-eye is a great stone to carry on any trip for its protective properties will comfort and soothe you while in unfamiliar surroundings.

ANIMALS.   Ladybugs are one of the animals of this area. They are quite beneficial to yards as well as being able to travel quickly and quietly. A ceramic ladybug would enhance this area quite nicely. Dragonflies add vitality and inspiration to travel plans and short-term relationships.

Bees, one of the most social creatures on the planet, enhance this area by bringing a feeling of community and celebration. Who can forget that mead is made possible by bees? Talk about a celebration! Generosity and nourishment are provided by the sow. We are definitely nourished by helpful people and other people's generosity, which is necessary for travel.

MUSICAL INSTRUMENTS.   If you play an instrument that is closely associated with another country, here would be the place to store it, especially if it is any kind of string or wind instrument.

HOLIDAYS.   Fun. Frolic. Fertility. In other words—Beltane. The first of May always revives us and brings us closer to people in our lives even if that closeness is only temporary. Making wishes for the future and celebrating the rites of spring all have a place in this Bagua area. Air feeds Fire. Stoke up the flames as much as you want in this area. You may find, however, that relationships formed in this area are fleeting. Mutual needs bring people together at Beltane and once those needs are met, they move on. Store your Maypole here or brightly colored ribbons. Place a vase full of fresh flowers in this area periodically, especially when you find yourself in need of a helpful person.

COLOR.   Orange is such a bright and cheerful color. It is also the color of sensuality, courage, and strength. Humor is revealed in a good belly laugh, the seat of orange. Revel in the fleeting relationships in your life and take sensual pleasure in your travels. Make a strong statement and paint that globe stand orange!

A huge orange candle with multiple wicks would also be good in this area. Orange is one of the colors of Fire to the south and by hanging wind chimes over it the heat rising from the lit candle will move the chimes thus manifesting the Air qualities of this area.

STAR RUNES.   The following Star Runes should be viewed in the color orange either by copying them onto orange paper or by tracing the actual symbol in orange.

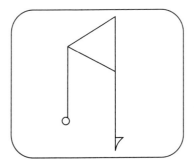

Figure 36. Joy, Desire, Delight
In our modern society, joy and delight are typically expressions reserved solely for children. It is considered immature to express these feelings in our lives. But, in listening to our desires, we find the courage to be joyful and to take delight in ourselves and the world around us.

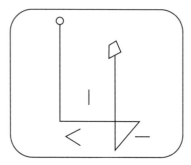

Figure 37. Elements of Creation, Conception

When all of the elements of creation are present, they must be brought together in such a way that allows conception to take place. Simply having all the elements does not guarantee conception. Action and organization must also exist.

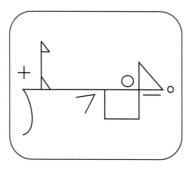

Figure 38. Relationship Building, Community, Diversity

Diversity is the key to relationship building. The best communities find strength in diversity. The strongest relationships are created from disparate elements. Even gold, the most precious metal on earth, is soft and unusable by itself. It becomes strong enough to use only when other metals are added.

NUMBER. Relationships are ruled by the number six. Social interactions, friendships and mentors are all present within the number six, so if you want that trip to Ireland, put up six photos or six maps of any size. Just remember, you must work for it mundanely as well as magickally!

TAROT. Now, let's go! Hitch up the horses and get your Chariot on down the road. Don't worry about those small rocks in your path. Wiccan Feng Shui will provide you with the momentum to blow them out of the way.

Consecration Ritual

Once you have chosen the enhancements for your Helpful People and Travel Bagua area, you will want to perform the following ritual to consecrate those items. This ritual is best done mid-morning, in between a Waxing and Full Moon since that is the time of day and moon cycle associated with SouthEast.

YOU WILL NEED:
Your athame
The red candle and the incense off your main altar
An orange candle

Choose a Goddess and God most closely associated with Beltane, Fire, Air, or both, or Travel. I will be presenting this ritual with Flora and Pan, but please feel free to change these to deities you work well with.

Prepare yourself as you would for any magickal working and prepare the space according to your traditions.

Facing SouthEast, invoke the Goddess and God asking them to be with you as you consecrate these sacred items.

Flora, Goddess of Fertility and Flowers.
Be with me to bless and consecrate these items so that they
*   may keep this dwelling alive with the power of*
*   cooperation and movement.*

So Mote It Be!

Pan, God of the Woods, Passion, and Fun.
Be with me to bless and consecrate these items so that they
*   may keep this dwelling alive with the power of*
*   cooperation and movement.*

So Mote It Be!

Light the candles. Call the elements of Fire to be present in the red and orange candles as you touch your athame to each in turn, and say:

Guardians of the South
Powers of Fire
Be with me to bless and consecrate these items so that they
*   may keep this dwelling alive with the power of Fire and*
*   the warmth of the Springtime sun.*

The light of your inspiration, courage, and love permeates
*   this* _____ [touch athame to chosen
enhancements].
Burn bright in my home for now and evermore.

Pass the enhancements through flame, and say:

I bless and consecrate these items with the Fire of the South.
May Helpful People and Travel reign within and outside of
*   my home.*

So Mote It Be!

Light the incense. Call the element of Air to be present in the orange candle and the incense as you touch your athame to each in turn, and say:

Guardians of the East,
Powers of Air,
Be with me to bless and consecrate these items so that they
*   may keep this dwelling alive with the power of*
*   cooperation and movement.*

The light of your creation, freshness, and clarity permeates
*   this* _____ [touch athame to chosen
enhancements].
Burn bright in my home for now and evermore.

Saturate the enhancements with the smoke from the incense, and say:

I bless and consecrate these items with the incense of the Air.
May Helpful People and Travel reign within and outside of my home.

So Mote It Be!

Thank you Guardians of the South,
Powers of Fire.
Go in Peace.

Thank you Guardians of the East,
Powers of Air,
Go in Peace.

Thank you Flora,
Go in Peace.

Thank you Pan,
Go in Peace.

It is done!

Let the orange candle burn until it goes out on its own. Your Bagua area of Helpful People and Travel is now set. The ritual is ended.

Magickal Workings

Now that the Helpful People and Travel area of your home is consecrated, you may wish to perform certain rituals or place specific items in this area that relate to Helpful People and

Travel. You can choose from the list below or add your own in the space provided.

Rituals for:
Fertility
Fun
Growth
Travel
Temporary partnerships
Community
Cooperation
Joint projects
Teamwork

My ideas:

Items:
Fresh flowers
Maps
Car keys
Board games and cards

NorthEast—Knowledge and Self-Cultivation

Imagine walking through a barren desert landscape. A hot wind is blowing and the grit and dust from the sandy desert floor is getting in your eyes and hair and feels as though it is tearing the top layer right off your skin. You blink constantly against the glare and your eyes feel gritty and dry. Your throat is parched and your lips are cracked and sore. You wonder if you will be able to survive and are about ready to give up when you spot a single tree in the distance. As you get closer you realize that it is an olive tree with a small pool of water at its base, providing you with those things you must have, shade and water. You rest with your back against the trunk. Once night falls, the desert comes to life and you realize that what you once thought was barren and dead is teeming with life and activity. You marvel at the simplicity of life and discover the higher purpose of the desert, to remove distractions from your life and scour your heart and soul clean.

Wiccan Feng Shui is that olive tree in the desert. It's no coincidence that prophets from many different religions have gone into the desert to be purified. They have returned with a clearer view of the world and an open heart. I had a similar experience several years ago, and I was in a car! Driving across the great desert of the American Southwest with no radio in my car and nothing to occupy my mind was an exhilarating experience after I got over the initial boredom. It changed me in ways that are still surfacing three years later!

Between Creativity and Children and Wealth and Prosperity lies the Bagua area of Knowledge and Self-Cultivation. It is in this area that we expand our minds and improve ourselves. Any and all kinds of study are ruled by this area, be it a mundane course from the local college or spiritual instruction from your High Priestess. It is also the area of improving our physical selves. It is in this area that we bridge the gap between mind and body. When these two areas of our lives are in harmony, it is then that we are open to the higher knowledge that comes in from Spirit.

The desert is a perfect metaphor for the Bagua area of Knowledge and Self-Cultivation between the firmness of the Earth beneath our feet and the hot wind of inspiration roaring in our ears. Any theme having to do with the desert is an excellent enhancement here. A cactus plant or, if you're into the southwestern flavor of decoration, a cow's skull with horns. When we reach the ultimate level of knowledge we are basically down to the bare bones of a subject. We've made it through all the flesh and meat and finally understand the underlying structure. Let your imagination roam with this one!

This would be an excellent place for your magickal library. Store your Book of Shadows here. If you are in school, place your desk here rather than in the career or wealth areas. Before beginning any course of study, enhance this area.

CRYSTALS.   Moonstone and clear quartz are the stones for this area. Moonstone, with its milky white depths, invites us to plunge in and discover its mysteries. Ever heard of Silicon Valley? The reason Silicon Valley is called that is because without silicon, most of our modern electronics could not exist. We depend on silicon for telephones, radios, satellites, computers, and fiber optics to name just a few. Quartz crystals consist of silicon dioxide, so it is not a great stretch of the imagination to consider using quartz in our magickal lives. They are crystals that receive, store and send information. Unlocking all their uses has filled several books so, suffice it to say, they are especially potent in this Bagua area, but can be used in all of them.

ANIMALS.   Butterflies are a great enhancement for this area for knowledge often transforms us, just as a caterpillar becomes a butterfly. Most burrowing animals are also appropriate here because, often, we must dig deep down in order to come to a full understanding of any subject.

The owl, raven, and crane are the trinity of birds that find a home in this Bagua area. The owl has long been a symbol of wisdom, but, in addition, the owl represents detachment and change. We must remain somewhat detached from our studies in order to remain objective about them, especially in magick. A belief in a predetermined outcome can very easily sway a spell one way or another, so we must step back and watch. Only then will we achieve our goal.

The call of the raven is the call to initiation. The raven is death and rebirth, just as the attainment of new knowledge can kill our old perceptions. Listen closely to the raven's prophetic call and you will discover the path you need to follow. The crane brings us the ability to focus patiently on our goals and brings the realization that the act of learning is just as important as the end result of knowledge gained. If you are embarking on the study of any of the Mysteries, call upon the crane. To the Druids, the crane symbolized arcane science and secret knowledge.

HOLIDAYS.   Just as Imbolc is all about light returning after the darkness of winter, this area is about the internal light being turned on. The light of self-realization. You must complete this step in life before venturing on to the Summerland and your next life. Some experience the light *after* death. Some just preceding. Imagine all the candles of the Imbolc crown being lit one by one over the course of your lifetime. Each one a lesson learned or knowledge gained. Once all the candles have been lit for this lifetime, they are brought together to form a brilliant bonfire that is your total life's work. You carry this light with you to the next life, where it appears as a single lit candle and you begin again.

COLOR.   The color for Knowledge and Self-Cultivation is clear or white, for white is the combination of all the colors in the rainbow. The underlying light in our Auric field is white and it completely surrounds and permeates our being.

STAR RUNES.   The following Star Rune should be viewed in the color white. A pearlized white on a black background is the most powerful way to display this symbol. Choose a color if you prefer. Just make sure that the color *truly* represents what you wish to learn.

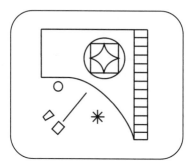

Figure 39. Balance

NUMBER.   The number five is the number of transition. All learning is a transition. Sometimes the transition is an easy one, sometimes not. It is no coincidence that a symbol of our faith—the pentacle—has five points.

TAROT.   This is the only Bagua area that has two Tarot trumps representing it, the Hermit and Death. The Hermit is the only way in which we truly gain knowledge in our lives. We may share our spiritual paths from time to time, but what we see along these paths is always uniquely our own. Once this knowledge has been gained, we go through a Death of old beliefs and are transformed. Keep the Hermit and Death in mind when doing rituals in this area and in all areas of your life that require learning.

Consecration Ritual

Once you have chosen the enhancements for your Knowledge and Self-Cultivation Bagua area, you will want to perform the following ritual to consecrate those items. This ritual is best done in between midnight and dawn, and between a Dark and Waxing Moon since that is the time of day and moon cycle associated with NorthEast.

YOU WILL NEED:
Your athame
The saucer of salt and the incense off your main
    altar
A white candle

Choose a Goddess and God most closely associated with Imbolc, Earth, Air or both, or with the course of study you are pursuing. I will be presenting this ritual with Al-Lat and Thoth, but please feel free to change these to deities you work well with.

Prepare yourself as you would for any magickal working and prepare the space according to your traditions.

Facing NorthEast, invoke the Goddess and God asking them to be with you as you consecrate these sacred items.

Al-Lat, Unshakable One, Goddess of the Desert.
Be with me to bless and consecrate these items so that they
    may keep this dwelling alive with the powers of
    Knowledge and Self-Cultivation.

So Mote It Be!

Thoth, God of Reincarnation, Wise One.
Be with me to bless and consecrate these items so that they
    may keep this dwelling alive with the powers of
    Knowledge and Self-Cultivation.

So Mote It Be!

Light the white candle. Call the elements of the North to be present in the candle and the salt as you touch your athame to each in turn, and say:

Guardians of the North,
Powers of Earth,
Be with me to bless and consecrate these items so that they
    may keep this dwelling alive with the powers of
    Knowledge and Self-Cultivation.

The light of your strength, stability, fertility, and growth
    permeates this _____ [touch athame to chosen
    enhancements].
Burn bright in my home and in my heart for now and
    evermore.

Sprinkle salt on the enhancements, and say:

I bless and consecrate these items with the salt of the Earth.
May Knowledge and Self-Cultivation be present within my
    home and my heart.

So Mote It Be!

Call the element of Air to be present in the candle and the
incense as you touch your athame to each in turn, and say:

Guardians of the East,
Powers of Air,
Be with me to bless and consecrate these items so that they
    may keep this dwelling alive with the powers of
    Knowledge and Self-Cultivation.

The light of your creation, freshness, and clarity permeates
    this _____ [touch athame to chosen
    enhancements].
Burn bright in my home and in my heart for now and
    evermore.

Saturate the enhancements with the smoke from the
incense, and say:

I bless and consecrate these items with the incense of the Air.
May knowledge and Self-Cultivation reign within my home
and my heart.

So Mote It Be!

Thank you Guardians of the East,
Powers of Air.
Go in Peace!

Thank you Guardians of the North,
Powers of Earth.
Go in Peace.

Thank you Al-Lat,
Go in Peace.

Thank you Thoth,
Go in Peace.

It is done!

Let the white candle burn until it goes out on its own. Your Bagua area of Knowledge and Self-Cultivation is now set.

The ritual is ended.

Magickal Workings

Now that the Knowledge and Self-Cultivation area of your home is consecrated, you may wish to perform certain rituals or place specific items in this area that relate to knowledge and self-cultivation. You can choose from the list below or add your own in the space provided.

Rituals for:
Study habits
Knowledge retention
Inspiration
Understanding
Initiation
Enlightenment
When feeling "in the dark"
    about anything

Items:
Books
Desk
Lamp (don't ever let it
    burn out!)
A perpetual candle
    (one that always
    burns)

My ideas:

3

GIVE ME ROOM

Now that we have examined each slice of the pie or Bagua area, it is time to look in our pantries and discover what ingredients we have to pull it all together. Each room is an ingredient in your house and not all houses are the same. Some have two living areas while others have only one. Does your house have two, three, or four bedrooms? Do you live in an efficiency apartment? Whatever the size or shape of your living space, we've got it covered, unless you live in a forty-room mansion. If so, give me a call! I do consulting.

Within each room lies a miniature Bagua. As a matter of fact, Bagua areas can be as small as a desk. Just overlay the Bagua map on a layout of a room instead of an entire dwelling to discover ways to enhance these areas, especially if you live in a one-room apartment. Speaking of which, if your living space is compact, you will need to designate "rooms" within rooms. Sometimes rooms have to be used for more than one purpose. When that is the case, be very careful how you arrange your furniture. After studying the Bagua map carefully, remember some general rules:

1. Keep your desk hidden from your bed or your main focus at home will be work.
2. Make your sleeping area a cozy little nest. Screens or large plants that enclose your sleeping area and block the view of the rest of the apartment work wonderfully here.
3. Bookcases are okay, but face the books toward your work or living area and not your bed.
4. If your table must also be a desk, designate one end of it as eating and the other end as working. Sit in the career or knowledge areas for work and leave the health area for eating.

I cannot say this strongly enough: USE EVERY ROOM IN YOUR HOUSE! Formal living or dining rooms that see activity only once or twice a year are a waste of space. Either use them as living or dining areas on a regular basis or change them into something else. A formal living room could become a game room or media center, getting the television out of the main living area. A formal dining room could be turned into a library or study. Turn it into an art studio and start painting again! If a room is not used on a regular basis, then the Chi in that room becomes stagnant and that Bagua area of your life will also become stagnant. Not good!

We are the Empress and Emperor of our homes, ruling the spaces inside them and determining how they are to be used. This is your kingdom. Make of it what you will (with the following tips, of course!).

Doors, Halls, and Stairs—Places of Transition

A day in the life. The alarm blares as you stumble out of bed and into the shower. After getting dressed, a cup of coffee jump-starts your day as you climb into the car and start your daily commute. After a long day at work, several errands must be run before returning home. As you walk in the front door, a heavy sigh releases your workday and you find yourself relaxing into home life. A nice dinner and quality time with family and friends ends your day. As you set your alarm and crawl into bed, the comfort of your home surrounds you and holds you tight until it is time to leave, once more, the next day.

Everything I just described is a transition. We tend to think of only major events in our lives as transitions: weddings, funerals, births, job changes, moving. The truth is we go through small transitions every day. The doors, halls, and stairs in our homes represent these transitions.

The front door is the transition between the outside world and our inner lives and as such, is the most important structure in the home. The front door should be prominent enough to stand out, yet fit the size of the house. A front door that is too large for the house may intimidate someone approaching it. On the other hand a very small door will not allow sufficient Chi to enter.

First things first. Go outside and look at your house from the street. Can you see your front door? If *you* can't, then neither can the Chi. Your front door should be obvious to any visitors. If you have two doors in the front and only use one of them, paint the one you don't use to blend in with the house and paint the one you do use to stand out. Double-door entryways may be impressive architecturally, but unless they both open on a regular basis, consider replacing them with a single door. It is bad Feng Shui to have a door that doesn't open. There are beautiful doorways that have stained or leaded glass panels on either side of a single opening door that fit double door openings. Whether you have a single or double door, make sure it opens all the way. If there is a table or umbrella stand preventing the door from fully opening, move it. This is the primary gateway for Chi to enter your house and it needs to do so entirely unimpeded.

If your front door is hidden from the street, make the walk a prominent part of your landscape. There should be no doubt how to reach the front door. Lining this walk with brightly colored flowers brightens your yard and encourages not only two-legged visitors, but also butterflies and beneficial insects. Flanking your front door with stone or concrete guardians like dragons, dogs, or elephants is highly recommended in traditional Feng Shui. For Wiccan Feng Shui, choose a totem animal instead. If you live in an apartment, a beautiful welcome mat or potted plant encourages the Chi to enter. If the hallway is dark, suspend a faceted crystal directly over your door. You'll be amazed at the difference it makes.

Before my husband and I bought a house, we lived in a wonderful open and airy apartment, but there was a problem. The hallway leading to our front door was dark and our door was directly across from our neighbors. You couldn't see the street or even the parking lot from our front door. The day I hung a faceted crystal in front of our door, the energy picked up and the fatigue I had been feeling for weeks began to dissipate. Make the entryway into your home as attractive as possible. Not only will it make you feel good upon arriving home, it encourages others to your door.

The following is the best Star Rune to have at your front door. It should be viewed in the color purple either by copying it onto purple paper or by tracing the actual symbol in purple.

Figure 40. Home, Contentment, Spiritual Pathways

At last we find through all our journeys outward that true contentment lies at home. Our spiritual pathways lead us to a better understanding of ourselves and the people around us. Our home is within us when we are content with ourselves.

Now stand in your front doorway and look out. What do you see? Are there any shars or poison arrows pointed at your door? Corners of buildings? Angled rooflines? A dead tree? Is your house located in a cul-de-sac or at the junction of a street or do you have a pretty view? All these things not only affect the way the world sees you, but also how you see the world. No matter how elegantly decorated and comfortable your home is, if your first view upon leaving it is a Dumpster or a junked car, the attitude created by that disharmony will affect the rest of your day.

While there's not much you can do about the last two things, short of calling a towing company, you can reflect the negativity back toward those items with a small round mirror hung directly over your front door. Now, about the view. A hedge or shrub will not only hide unsightly items from your view, it will slow down rushing Chi if your house is located in a cul-de-sac or at a T intersection. Remember, Chi flows like a river down streets and if one ends at your driveway or front door, you may find yourself swept away by too much Chi entering your home.

An attached garage is just as much a part of your house as any other room. If it is under the same roof, it is included in the Bagua areas. A detached garage does not carry the same importance and acts more as a storage facility. The best placement for a garage is to the rear of the house so it does not compete with the front door. A garage facing the street should be painted the same color as the house so the Chi knows that the front door is the main entrance.

This Star Rune is best in your garage. It should be viewed in the color red either by copying it onto red paper or by tracing the actual symbol in red.

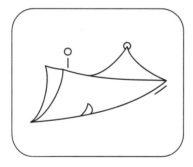

Figure 41. Travel, Direction, Transportation

Movement in our daily lives brings a sense of purpose to everyday activities. But, we must have a direction to travel before we can progress towards the realization that we are not static beings, even if we only travel within ourselves.

If, like me, you almost always enter the house through an interior garage door, then make that entryway just as beautiful and pleasing to the eye as your front door. Let's face it, most of us that have garages leave them pretty junked out and I'm just as guilty as the next person. It is a chore keeping up with the clutter, especially if you are into crafts or hobbies that take place in the garage. Just try to make the first thing you see something that uplifts your soul and gladdens your heart. I painted the garage side of the door leading into my home with a special paint, turning that door into a chalkboard. I keep a bucket of sidewalk chalk next to it and I change the view frequently. One day it is a landscape and the next day my hubby and I leave each other silly notes. The great thing about that is no one sees it but us! It can get pretty steamy in there from time to time if you know what I mean!

In which Bagua area of your home is your front door located? This has great significance to the overall energy of the house because the Chi is flavored by the Bagua area it is passing through. If your front door faces North, then Wealth and Prosperity will be the primary concern in your home. If it faces East, your Creativity and Children will be of the utmost importance. Keep this in mind when searching for a place to live, be it a new house, apartment, or loft. If you are already firmly planted and discover that your front door is located in a Bagua area that you would rather not emphasize in your life, there is something you can do other than move.

If work seems to be dominating your life, you may find that your front door faces NorthWest; the Career area of the Bagua. Since you need your career, you don't want to de-emphasize this area, but instead, build a shrine to it. Place the enhancements that you have chosen for this area just inside your front door, preferably within something that can be closed. A wooden cabinet or box is a good choice. When you leave for work in the morning open the box and when you get home at night, close it. This simple act keeps the energy of your career strong, but hides it from your home life. It still exists within your home, but it is no longer the primary emphasis. You could combine this with the ritual found in the NorthWest—Career section (page 88) and you will definitely find that work no longer dominates your life.

On to the interior. Stand within your front door and face inside the house. Can you see the back door from where you stand? Bad news! If *you* can then the Chi can. It will flow in the front door and immediately out the back. We need to keep that Chi circulating in the house. Screen that view with plants or place another one of those marvelously helpful faceted crystals just inside the front door to disperse the Chi. Chi, like any river, also has a hard time making sharp turns. Help it along with chimes, plants, or mirrors

Speaking of rivers . . . If you have stairs in your home, you also have a waterfall. Chi rushes very quickly down stairs, so if your front door opens directly onto a staircase, all the Chi could be flowing right out the front door every time someone enters or leaves. Ouch. The stairs in that position also make people entering the home feel uneasy, as if something is looming over them, especially if the stairs go directly up with no landing. Small plants placed every few steps can help slow down the Chi. If your stairs are too narrow for that, place a piece of artwork at the bottom or better yet, hang art in a straight horizontal line about halfway up. Whatever you do, never hang art in a descending line; this encourages the Chi to flow even faster.

Doors within the home should never be opposite one another. When they are you get into a Ping-Pong match with the Chi and—I'm aging myself here—like the original computer Pong game, if you get it going just right, you can leave and it will just keep going back and forth. Nothing fresh enters those rooms and it makes any negativity harder to get rid of. A small mirror over one of the doors angled just slightly away will keep the Chi flowing. You want to make sure enough energy gets into *all* the rooms of the house.

Long hallways are similar to stairs in that they move the Chi along at an accelerated rate. To slow it down, group pictures or objects at various places along the hall. Keep each grouping an island unto itself, this forces the Chi to stop and get a taste of each section, so it slows down long enough to meander into the rooms. This is one place where a mirror is *not* a good idea. Placing a mirror at the end of a hall makes it feel even longer; then the Chi really gets confused.

Any ritual that helps transitions occur will be enhanced if performed in a hall or on the stairs. It is no coincidence that brides often come down a stairway at the beginning of a wedding ceremony. Symbolically, they are making the transition from one level of their life to the next.

Tarot trump of the fool represents the doors, halls, and stairs in our lives by standing at the edge of new adventure and entering that adventure with the innocence of a child. Just remember to put solid ground on the other side of those doors. The following sections will help with that task.

Living Room—Alive with Activity

It's the day of the big game. Friends and family members have arrived. Some are gathered around the television cheering on their teams while others are bringing in snacks from the kitchen. In the corner of the living room several kids are coloring and two friends are sitting on the hearth having a serious heart to heart. During the afternoon, conversation partners change several times and everything from A to Z is discussed. After the game, the kids put on a short play for the adults then they shuffle off to bed, leaving the adults to settle in for the evening. An impromptu game of dominoes is started that lasts well into the evening until, at last, farewells are made and guests go to their own homes and beds. In the midst of all this activity is a feeling of warmth and belonging.

The living room is the most public room in the house. It's where we entertain not only others but ourselves as well. It is the central room that houses our hopes and aspirations. It's a room of doing and being. It reflects the melding of all the tastes in the family. It's where the family comes together most often, whether it is to watch a favorite TV program, play games, or just sit and talk. With that in mind, we need our main living space, be it den, family room, game room, or formal living room to act a little like a chameleon.

First of all, whether we like to admit it or not, the focus of most living rooms is the television set. This is positive Feng Shui when it is on for it brings positive Chi into the room because of the light and movement on the screen. But when the TV is off, it is a big blank eye and people feel uncomfortable being stared at. To encourage conversation and activities other than TV watching, consider an entertainment center with doors that close when the TV is not in use. If you don't like that idea, try placing a bright scarf over it when it's off or stack floor pillows in front of it. Lean a giant pillow against it. Not only does this block the blank eye, it also gives a comfortable backrest to someone who prefers sitting on the floor and completes a circle in terms of conversation.

Speaking of circles, I chose a large round, red rug for my main living area. The couch is on one side, next is a chair and ottoman, with a coffee table in the center. The roundness of the rug not only deflects the shars from the corners of the coffee table inside it and the shars of the hearth to one side of it, it encourages conversation and the red color is energizing and stabilizing. During my housewarming party, I was pleased to see people pull chairs up just to the edge of this rug in order to join the conversation. Most of the guests had left by this time and the dozen that remained were all close friends, so it was not surprising that we had come together in a circle. And boy was that conversation fun!

If the space is large enough, try creating several individual areas in one. In my home, I have three distinct areas in my living room. There's the middle where the fireplace is the main focus and that red rug is located. In the corner there is a table than can be used for eating or games and then against one wall are two chairs separated by a small end table where a more private conversation can occur. This area is also where the phone is located, so while having a phone conversation, you can almost feel the person on the other end of the line sitting in the chair next to you.

I mentioned the fireplace. The hearth. The centerpiece of the room. It's best to make the fireplace a focal point, but not at the expense of conversation. Make sure there are ways for people to look at one another while seated around the fire. If possible, create a circular conversation area around your fireplace with the seating far enough away that no one feels as if they are "getting burned" or arguments may erupt. Fireplaces are wonderful additions to any house, but the Chi can get pulled right out of the flue when it is not in use. The traditional remedy to this is to place a mirror over the fireplace to bounce the Chi back into the room. This adds a traditional and formal touch to your living room. If you would prefer something else over your fireplace, then use the screen technique described in the section on bathrooms (page 160) that I use to cover sinks and toilets.

Other than general conversation areas, seating in the living room should always be comfortable. Flat wooden chairs with stiff backs are not conducive to lounging, but then again neither are sofas so soft that you sink into them so far you need a crane to pull you out. Try to avoid arranging furniture that would put someone's back to the door. This makes people feel uncomfortable and anxious. If, because of your floor plan, this situation is unavoidable, then you as host, should always offer to sit in that spot.

Pull your furniture away from the edges of the rooms. Our tendency is to push all the furniture up against the walls, leaving a big open space in the middle of the room. This is fine if you want to install a hoop over the fireplace and play basketball later, but this is the living room, the most public room in the house. It's where the family comes together and friends are made to feel like family. Bring them close and make them part of the action. Put them in the center of things, as it were, instead of on the sidelines watching the game.

Just as people are uncomfortable with their backs to the door, the same is true if their backs are to windows. It creates a feeling of being unsupported. This can be difficult, especially if your living room is full of windows, as mine is. The best remedy for this situation is not to back everyone up against the wall, but to put something solid and substantial behind the seating areas. This is how sofa tables are used. Placed behind the sofa, it gives a feeling of stability. Plants are also good for this purpose as are short or tall screens. And don't be afraid to rearrange your furniture every once in a while. Change is healthy and helps you to see things in a new light. If a piece of furniture is simply not working in your living room, relegate it to another room in the house or find another creative use for it. If it doesn't seem to fit in anywhere, it might be best to get rid of it. If *it* is not comfortable in the house, *you* won't be comfortable having it in the house.

Examine your wants for this area. Do you prefer intellectual discourse? Then fill your living room with books and large splashes of yellow for clear creative thought. Do you prefer a more laid-back atmosphere where relaxation is the primary concern? Then place big fluffy floor pillows everywhere in shades of blue and green. If your primary focus is entertaining, make sure the colors are bright and lively. Reds and oranges will keep people active and moving around, which is what you want during any party. Just make sure you have a calmer space available, a seating area in another room for example, as an oasis from all the activity.

All the elements are appropriate in the living room depending on how you wish to use this space. Earth keeps everyone grounded, Water provides emotional comfort, Fire keeps things lively, and Air encourages conversation. Mix and match at will.

If the family room or den is the most used room in the house and you have a formal living room that is not used much, think of a way to incorporate this unused space into your life. Turn it into a library or study or make it a game room. Gone are the days of rooms used only for company. Most houses being built these days have a giant great room and no formal living room. Or if there is a formal living room, it is small and usually set away from the main traffic areas. Whatever your set up, USE EVERY ROOM IN YOUR HOUSE! Let no area stagnate. A room used only once a month or a few times a year is a waste of space and an area in your life AND a Bagua area that is being ignored. Like seldom used muscles, you will soon find those areas in your life weak and unsupported.

The best Bagua areas for your living room are the ones that involve other people in your life. The Health and Family area is an auspicious place for your living room, bringing close friends and family even closer while nurturing good health among all. If entertaining is your thing, then your parties will be the hit of the social scene if your living room is in the Fame and Reputation area. Do you prefer smaller, more intimate parties? Then the South is the best place for your living room, a place where couples will feel the most at home. Your living room is greatly enhanced if it is located in one of these three areas. If your living room is located in the very center of your house, even better, as it becomes the center of your universe!

All types of rituals are appropriate in your living room because it represents a melding of all aspects of your life. I know many Witches who move the furniture and cast their circle in the middle of their living rooms for *every* Sabbat and Esbat.

The following Star Runes will enhance your main living area. The first two should be viewed in the color orange either by copying them onto orange paper or by tracing the actual symbol in orange.

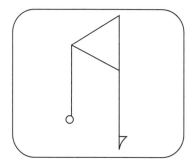

Figure 42. Joy, Desire, Delight

In our modern society, joy and delight are typically expressions reserved solely for children. It is considered immature to express these feelings in our lives. But, in listening to our desires, we find the courage to be joyful and to take delight in ourselves and the world around us.

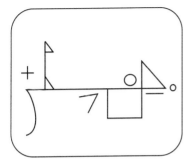

Figure 43. Relationship Building, Community, Diversity

Diversity is the key to relationship building. The best communities find strength in diversity. The strongest relationships are created from disparate elements. Even gold, the most precious metal on earth, is soft and unusable by itself. It becomes strong enough to use only when other metals are added.

The next Star Rune should be viewed in the color light blue either by copying it onto light blue paper or by tracing the actual symbol in light blue.

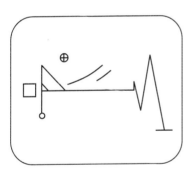

Figure 44. Multisource Information

Information from only one source always leaves us with a skewed perspective. Wading through and disseminating information from many different sources brings us closer to truth and understanding. Focus on this Star Rune to help you break down massive amounts of information.

The next Star Rune should be viewed in the color yellow either by copying it onto yellow paper or by tracing the actual symbol in yellow.

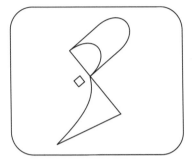

Figure 45. Power, Perpetual Motion

One of the great truths of the universe is the saying (and I'm paraphrasing here): "Objects at rest or in motion tend to stay that way until acted upon by an outside force." That outside force doesn't have to be physical. We often need to ask for a push to get us going, whether from a spirit guide or from our own higher selves. And once we have motion, it becomes perpetual, constantly renewing our power.

Strength is the Tarot trump for the living room for when the family comes together and shares interests, a unified front is presented to the world. Fold up that strength and put it in your pocket.

Your living room reflects your personality to the world as well as bringing your family closer together. Make this active room one that you enjoy spending time in and one that doesn't just revolve around the TV set. Be comfortable, be happy, and fill this room with the things that everyone in the family enjoys. Then use those enjoyments to entertain the world in your living room.

Kitchen—Heart of the Home

It's the night of the big party and the house has been scoured down to the tiniest detail. There are decorative fingertip towels in the bathroom. Scented candles are lit throughout the house and the aroma wafts from room to room. A fire is roaring in the fireplace and a beautiful tray of hors d'oeuvres sits on the coffee table untouched. The bar in the dining room has been visited just long enough for guests to refill their glasses and head back to the rest of the group . . . standing in the kitchen.

It never fails. No matter how elegantly your living room is decorated or how beautifully your dining room table is set, most of the guests at any party still end up in the kitchen. And it's not just because the host is in there, it's because the kitchen is the heart of the house. The kitchen is nourishing like the dining room, nurturing like the bedroom, but active like the living room. We show our love for others by preparing food. Great cooks are inspired and productivity is the name of the game. But the kitchen is always a place of transition for we rarely sit and relax while in the kitchen. Everything done in a kitchen has a purpose. You could say that the kitchen is the most purposeful room in the house. Do you ever go to the kitchen just to hang out if no one else is at home? Unlikely. We go there to get something to nourish ourselves or others, and even if you don't like to cook, the kitchen is where food and eating utensils are stored, so it always has nurturing qualities.

No matter where in the Bagua your kitchen is located, it is important to balance all the elements equally for it contains elements of all the other rooms in your house. A rainbow theme is an excellent choice for a kitchen. If you want to be more creative in your cooking, paint the walls yellow and add splashes of indigo for health. Go lightly on reds and oranges however, because there is already so much Fire energy present in the stove, oven, microwave, and toaster.

An aloe vera plant is a wonderful addition to any kitchen for several reasons: the physical effect of healing burns and cuts, the green growing enhancement for Wealth and Prosperity, and the magickal properties of Water. Keeping the plant near your sink will help keep water flowing freely through the pipes. No need for drain cleaner in *your* kitchen! The magickal properties of aloe also help to counterbalance the abundance of Fire energy in the kitchen.

It is best if the refrigerator is opposite the stove, keeping the hot and cold elements balanced. If the fridge is beside the stove/oven, perform the following ritual. Take a single terminated crystal, hold it in your right hand and recite this chant:

With my will I program
This crystal, to cause a door to slam
Between hot and cold
Do not fold
Stay steady and true
Crystal I imbue

Then place the crystal somewhere between the stove/oven and fridge. This way the hot and cold energies won't leak over into one another.

Without this barrier you might find that the fridge doesn't keep things very cold or the stove/oven won't get very hot or keeps breaking down. This ritual also works if the sink and stove are next to each other. Be careful not to sweep the crystal away during cleaning!

Cleanliness is extra important in the kitchen because nasty germs tend to thrive and multiply wherever there might be food remains. Keep your fridge cleaned out. Don't allow science projects to form on the bottom shelf for this invites illness into your home. It's best to keep your trash bin under the sink or otherwise hidden. If it must be out in the open, make sure it has a lid to keep the refuse contained. Along these same lines, NEVER put a cat's litter box in the kitchen because the energy of human or animal waste is a major detriment to the healthy aspects of the kitchen. If your house has two stories, double-check the locations of any bathrooms above the kitchen. Perform a ritual similar to the one between the stove and refrigerator if a toilet is directly above the kitchen or a dining room. It is imperative to keep these energies separate!

If you're trying to stay on a special diet due to illness or for weight loss, write your goal on a piece of indigo colored paper and place it in the West of your kitchen for Health. Use only positive goals. Refrain from putting a picture of yourself on the fridge that reminds you of how fat you are. No good. You'll only reinforce that unwanted image of yourself and that is counter-productive to your goal. Keeping your pantry and refrigerator well stocked shows the Universe that food is always avail-able, you are well nourished and that extra food is unneeded in your life.

Keep clutter to a minimum on kitchen counters. If you don't have room to spread out and cook, you'll find yourself not wanting to cook at all! If your kitchen is large enough to boast a table, try not to use that table as a catchall for mail, books, newspapers, and so on. Keeping your kitchen table clear invites fellowship in and goes a long way to keeping the rest of your house clear as well. If you must put mail in the kitchen, designate a basket that can easily be picked up and moved.

Since so much revolves around the kitchen, it would behoove you to dedicate a shrine to a hearth God or Goddess. Bridget is a wonderful Goddess for your kitchen, for not only is she a Fire Goddess, she is also a Goddess of healing and inspi-ration. Make this shrine a simple one; by using a single candle or image because, like I said earlier, clutter needs to be kept to a minimum. Dedicating your entire kitchen to a specific deity will transform your kitchen and everything you do in it into a magickal act.

A well-lit cheerful kitchen is essential to good Feng Shui. Besides the obvious of seeing what you are working on, bright light dispels gloom and shadows that could find their way into your food.

You should also rotate your use of the burners on the stove. Doing this shows the Universe that you want variety in your life as well as inspiration from many different sources. If a burner doesn't work, get it fixed or you may find an avenue in your life blocked. It is essential that everything in the kitchen be in good working order. If something doesn't work, remove it from your kitchen immediately. It is unhealthy to keep non-working items in your home in general and the kitchen in particular. If you plan on fixing the item, do so as soon as possible or store it away in an unseen corner of a closet until you can. Otherwise, get rid of it. There are many charities that take non-working items and repair them for resale.

Mirrors over the stove provide two positive Feng Shui roles; they allow you to see behind you and they multiply the healthy energies of the food being prepared. Being startled while cooking is like dropping an unwashed onion into a batch of cookies. Yuck! Not only does the taste suffer, so does the healthiness of the food. Being able to see behind you can prevent this. If you practice Kitchen witchery (which we all do to one extent or another), mirrors also increase the power of any spells you are working with the food.

The kitchen is also a marvelous place to do any ritual relating to health, well-being, prosperity and friendship. If your kitchen happens to be in the SouthWest corner of your house, you may find your dinner parties becoming the hit of the neighborhood since the direction of the SouthWest represents Fame and Reputation. The best Bagua area for your kitchen is in the West, the area of Health and Family. If you like to experiment with new dishes or involve your children in the preparation of meals then the East, the Bagua area of Creativity and Children is best. Don't despair if your kitchen is in another Bagua area, simply enhance the East or West areas of your kitchen to receive their full benefits. Remember, within each room is a miniature Bagua.

These two Star Runes are great kitchen helpers. The first one should be viewed in the color orange either by copying it onto orange paper or by tracing the actual symbol in orange.

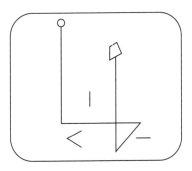

Figure 46. Elements of Creation, Conception

When all of the elements of creation are present, they must be brought together in such a way that allows conception to take place. Simply having all the elements does not guarantee conception. Action and organization must also exist.

The second Star Rune should be viewed in the color green either by copying it onto green paper or by tracing the actual symbol in green.

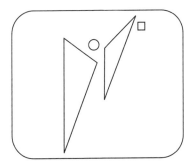

Figure 47. Health, Emotional Strength

Physical health is the best path to emotional strength. This Star Rune is a reminder that true wealth is achieved only when mind, body, and spirit are in balance.

My husband, who doesn't cook, says that cooking reminds him of alchemy; taking several unrelated items and transforming them into something new. He's right, of course. That is exactly what cooking is! We are all magicians when it comes to preparing meals, so the Tarot trump of the Magician rules the kitchen.

In ancient times, the hearth was the center of the house. In modern times, that honor has moved to the living room or den, but our souls remember gathering around the fireplace to keep warm while we awaited the meal that was cooking over that same fire. Take care of the kitchen, keep it clean, well lit and cheerful, and these qualities will spill over into the rest of the house.

Dining Room—Nourishing Space

The table is set with silk cloths and bone china. The fine crystal and flatware is shining in the glow from the candles set into your silver candlesticks. The aroma of a delicious meal wafts in from the kitchen enticing the palate of all present. As the first dishes are brought to the table, an appreciative hush descends over those assembled and the bearer of these platters flushes with pride. The meal is savored and complimented until the final dessert spoon has been laid aside. Fresh ground coffee is served as the conversation livens and you realize that this is a perfect moment in time, one full of friendship and laughter and you decide you never want it to end. In fact, you decide that this is the way all meals in your home will be served from now on.

Yeah. Right.

Okay, now for a dose of reality. You rush in from work, exhausted because the boss cut your deadline in half, the freeway was a parking lot and you couldn't bear the thought of making one more stop at the grocery store. Not after already stopping at the card shop, the cleaners, the shoe repair place, and the bank. You scour the pantry for something to throw together and manage the remarkable feat of a meal made out of nothing. Talk about magick! Just as you think about putting the meal down on your dining room table, you remember that your favorite show is on tonight, so you balance your plate on your lap and settle in front of the TV vowing that, one day, you'll use your dining room table as a *dining room table* and not as a desk, craft table, science project area, mail basket.

Do I exaggerate? Of course! The truth is probably somewhere in between these two extremes although we touch on both during the course of our daily lives. There was an old commercial where two people decide to eat their frozen meal in the dining room and one says to the other, "So, this is the dining room." The dining room in most homes is the most formal and least used room in the house. The table becomes a catchall for whatever projects are currently under way. Most of us eat at the kitchen table or in front of the television. If you only use your dining room for meals once or twice a year, then it is time to redesignate the space (see page 47) and designate the kitchen table or breakfast bar as your primary eating space. Whatever you do, try to use this space *only* for meals.

In our fast-paced society, eating has been relegated to something that is done to survive and only occasionally do we spend our eating times simply enjoying our food. We pay bills, read a book, talk on the phone, or discuss business. I've been guilty of all of these. I'm not saying that we must completely interrupt our lives for our meals, however (you knew there was going to be a however), it has been suggested by many in the field of health—Deepak Chopra among them—that we better digest our meals and pull more nutrition out of food when we eat purposefully, concentrating on the food itself. Aroma, texture, and taste are all designed for our enjoyment, and from our enjoyment comes our nourishment.

With that in mind, the focus in the dining room should be primarily on the food on the table. Keep decorations to a minimum. A dining room that is filled with too much to look at takes away from the food. It is best if the only furniture in the room is the table and chairs. A small, simple sideboard is okay, too. The elaborate glass breakfronts that allow you to show off your fine crystal and china actually create an uncomfortable atmosphere in the dining room, for your guests feel crowded and are unlikely to linger for conversation. If you have a piece of furniture of this type consider moving it to the living room. This way your beautiful possessions are still on display, but they are no longer "looking over someone's shoulder" while they eat.

King Arthur must have been a student of Feng Shui! Round is the best shape for a dining room table. It makes everyone at the table feel welcome and equally important since there is no "head." The energy flows gently around a round table and it also emulates a sacred circle. Square and rectangular tables not only have sharp corners or shars, but can also create an adversarial atmosphere as guests are "facing off" across the table. If you do have a square or rectangular table, NEVER seat anyone at a corner. The shar pointing directly at their stomach can cause severe digestive problems.

The elements of Fire and Water coexist perfectly in this room. The fire and warmth of the food brings forth the warmth of friendship while gently flowing waters encourage good-natured conversation and fine health. A perfect Fire enhancement for this room is one that has commonly been used for centuries: candles. Candles have evolved from a necessary source of light to the more subtle application of creating atmosphere. Candles in the middle of the table or in sconces along the walls are an excellent and simple way to bring warmth to the dining room.

A painting of the ocean or a mountain stream will not only enhance the beauty of the room, but it will also enhance the Water element and bring health into the room. Photos of flowing waters as well as the colors of blue and green also aid digestion and sooth frayed nerves. What better colors for a dining room especially after a hectic day!

The secondary focus of the dining room is the family sitting around the table. Breaking bread together was, at one time, considered to be the highest compliment you could give another person. It showed your willingness to share what you worked so hard to acquire—the food—and your guest showed an enormous amount of trust in eating something prepared without his or her supervision. So when we invite others to our table, we make them a part of our family, if only temporarily.

Make this room warm and inviting and the chairs comfortable to linger in. If your dining room is in the front of your house, try to block everyone's view of the front door or people will have a tendency to "eat and run." A well placed plant or folding screen works well in this instance. The same items can be used to create a separate "room" if your eating and living area are one big space. A dining room should be cozy, as if you are lying in the arms of the Goddess, safe, protected, and loved. It is best if there are two entrances to the dining room as the Chi flows in and out more easily emulating the food flowing in and waste carried out of your body.

Through sympathetic magick (which means using a physical representation for magickal intent), mirrors not only symbolically double the food on the table, but also the number of friends in your life. A large mirror or mirrored wall is perfect for the dining room; decorative, yet it does not detract from the main focus of the food.

Speaking of friends. Always have at least one empty chair at your table. This encourages visitors, both magickally and mundanely. This way you don't have to go hunting for a chair should someone stop by. We are, by nature, creatures of habit. We have set routines and, although they sometimes feel constricting, these routines are a comfort in our lives. However, when it comes to the dining room, it is a good idea to break with routine and change the chair in which you always sit every once in a while. Doing this helps the Chi flow more easily around the room and also encourages visitors. An extra chair never sat in becomes stagnant and unappealing.

Rituals for Health and Friendship are enhanced if done in the dining room, as are rituals for Wealth and Prosperity. In ancient times abundant food could mean the difference between life and death and represents Wealth even in our modern times, so the dining room is greatly enhanced if it is located in the Wealth and Prosperity Bagua area. The Health and Family Bagua area is also an excellent location for your dining room, bringing your family closer together and increasing the healthy aspects of the food you are eating. If elaborate dinner parties are your thing, look for a home with the dining room in the Fame and Reputation area and your efforts will be greatly appreciated and talked about.

The following Star Runes will help make your meals magickal. The first two should be viewed in the color orange either by copying them onto orange paper or by tracing the actual symbol in orange.

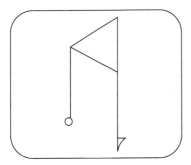

Figure 48. Joy, Desire, Delight

In our modern society, joy and delight are typically expressions reserved solely for children. it is considered immature to express these feelings in our lives, but, in listening to our desires, we find the courage to be joyful and to take delight in ourselves and the world around us.

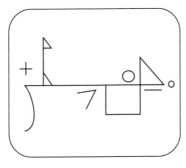

Figure 49. Relationship Building, Community, Diversity

Diversity is the key to relationship building. The best communities find strength in diversity. The strongest relationships are created from disparate elements. Even gold, the most precious metal on earth, is soft and unusable by itself. It becomes strong enough to use only when other metals are added.

The next Star Rune should be viewed in the color green either by copying it onto green paper or by tracing the actual symbol in green.

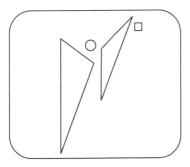

Figure 50. Health, Emotional Strength

Physical health is the best path to emotional strength. This Star Rune is a reminder that true wealth is achieved only when mind, body, and spirit are in balance.

The last Star Rune for the dining room should be viewed in the color light blue either by copying it onto light blue paper or by tracing the actual symbol in light blue.

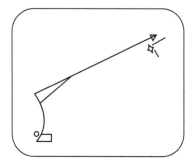

Figure 51. Service to Others, Speaking Out, Justice

True justice lies not in others or in a governmental system. True justice lies in speaking out our truths, whatever they may be, without attachment to the final outcome. In this way, we truly serve others and ourselves. For courage in speaking your mind to others use this Star Rune as a focus. The best dinner conversations are ones that lean toward the controversial.

Temperance is the Tarot trump for the dining room, for it reminds us that everything, but especially food, should be taken in moderation. Like the Lady pouring out water to nourish the land our dining room is one of two rooms in the house (the other is the kitchen) that continually nourishes us. It is in the dining room that we transform our food into energy for our bodies.

Remember, try to take time to eat for eating's sake. Rushing through meals not only causes indigestion, it dishonors the food being consumed. Honor your food and the room in which you eat it and you honor your body with sustained energy and abundant nutrition.

Bedroom—Love and Relaxation

Mom's bed. It held an array of cousins at Thanksgiving and loads of clothes fresh from the dryer on any other given day. It was where I learned (via encyclopedia) about the birds and the bees. When I wanted a private phone conversation, Mom's bedroom is where I held it. As a matter of fact, all private conversations took place on Mom's bed from discussions about low grades to comfort over broken hearts. When Mom's door was shut with one of us inside, no interruption was permitted. Tears of joy and tears of pain soiled the sheets of Mom's bed. It was king size and dominated the room. There was barely enough room for a dresser, two nightstands, and the ironing board that never seemed to get put away. But it was filled to overflowing with love and understanding.

In no other room do we express love as intimately: physically, emotionally, and spiritually. We dream our highest dreams in our bedroom and no wish is ever thought to be too outrageous.

The bedroom is an interesting mix of activity and relaxation. The most obvious purpose of a bedroom is sleep. The second is sex. Both these activities nourish our souls in completely different ways. Or are they that different? Feelings of contentment and relaxation follow each of these activities. We emerge from our beds feeling rested and rejuvenated, no matter which activity was taking our time while there.

Since the bedroom is all about emotions, it is a good place to have an aquarium or small fountain. I know I sleep exceptionally well when it is raining outside, so the gentle sounds of a fountain can lull you into deep sleep. Water elements in general add to the effectiveness of the Chi in your bedroom, just make sure you place it in the western portion of the room.

"Steamy" has been used to describe sexy movies and intense love affairs. There's a reason for this description. We know that Water is a good enhancement to any bedroom because of its emotionally calming properties. Add Fire for Love and Marriage and you've got steam. The best placement for your master bedroom is in the South for Love and Marriage if you're coupled, or in the West for Health and Family if you're single. A good way to attract a mate is to enhance the southern area of your bedroom with two objects of like size. See the chapter on the Bagua area of Love and Marriage for more ways to enhance this area (page 69). Love spells are the most effective if performed in the southern area of your bedroom.

Keep the colors in your bedroom cool: blues, greens, deep purples. These are relaxing colors. Reds, oranges, and yellows are too active for bedrooms in general, but if used sparingly they will increase the passion of the room. I have stoppered candles in warm colors in my bedroom. Not only does the candlelight add to an enjoyable sexual experience, but removing the stoppers readies the room magickally for lovemaking.

Color in children's bedroom is especially important and from the time we are babies our environments are affecting us. There's something to be said for the adage, "Blue is for boys. Pink is for girls." Since boys tend to be more active, blue calms them down. Pink is a nurturing color so we automatically think of little girls. If you have a hyperactive child, try painting that child's room in cool, soothing colors. Stay away from bright, primary colors and stick to pastels. If your child is prone to depression, warm, bright colors are a definite plus, especially yellow. Just be careful not to overuse reds and oranges or you'll never get your child to sleep!

I'm sure you have all heard the expression; "Getting up on the wrong side of the bed." The way we greet each day determines our moods and attitudes toward the rest of the day. With this in mind, it is important to place a pleasing object within sight immediately upon awakening and to decorate your bedroom in a way that makes you feel comforted and safe.

I know that under-the-bed storage boxes are all the rage, but it is really not a good idea to store things under the bed. All objects hold energy. Ask any psychomotrist. As Witches, we intentionally put energy into tools by consecrating them, but we sometimes forget that everything around us receives the energies we put out on a constant basis. Even clothes. So try not to store anything under your bed and keep the dust bunnies swept out or you may find that your sleep is disturbed by bits and pieces of dreams unrelated to your life.

At the beginning of this section, I spoke about multi-purpose rooms. Those same rules apply here. If you must have a desk or workout machine in your bedroom, hide it when you sleep. This can be accomplished by the use of screens or draperies. Remember, your bedroom's primary function is relaxation and it's difficult to relax with a pile of work glaring at you from your desk. Working out in your bedroom actually stimulates the flow of Chi and increases the general healthfulness of the room, but an *unused* piece of equipment only serves to make you feel guilty and guilt is a negative motivator. It may work, but there are other motivations that are more positive. Like most things in your house, "if you don't use it, lose it!"

Mirrors bounce energy. In any other room of the house it is beneficial to use mirrors to direct Chi. In the bedroom, however, mirrors can have a detrimental effect. If you happen to glimpse your reflection in a mirror in the middle of the night, your subconscious mind might think that there is someone else in the room with you or you are seeing your own ghost. This is not good for your peace of mind. If you must have mirrors in your bedroom, try to angle them away from your bed or better yet, cover them at night. I have a full-length mirror opposite my bed that I draped like a window. I pull aside the drape during the day and close it at night so I'm not startled by my reflection.

The best ways to move Chi in your bedroom are with plants and wind chimes, not mirrors.

The placement of your bed is also of great importance. Just like in the living room, you don't want to have your back to the door. In all instances try to face the door, but without your feet pointing directly out the door. This position is known in traditional Feng Shui as the death position because corpses were lined up with the door in this way to provide them easier access to the afterworld. So unless you're dead (dead tired doesn't count) avoid placing your bed in this position. In the following illustration, there are also two shars that intersect the bed, one from the corner of the dresser, the other from the corner of the nightstand. Sleeping with a shar pointing directly at you can be detrimental to your health.

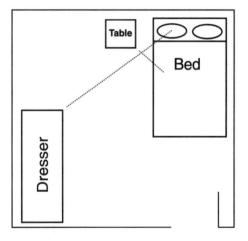

Figure 52. Death Bed Position

The ideal location for your bed is angled in a corner facing the door. The bed is in its position of power with a small table at the head to lend stability. It keeps your water glass handy, too! The shars from the table and the dresser are pointing away from the bed and adding a plant in the corner encourages the Chi to circulate throughout the room.

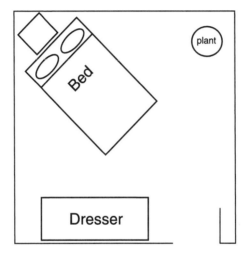

Figure 53. Bedroom Corrections

If your room is not big enough for this type of arrangement, then place the head of the bed on the wall opposite the door as opposed to the same wall.

I talked earlier about overhead beams. The placement of beams in the bedroom is of utmost importance since a third of your life is spent sleeping. It is best if there are no overhead beams at all in your bedroom. If a beam runs down the center of your bed from head to foot, you could experience marital or relationship problems. If a beam runs side to side over your bed, your health could be negatively affected. If you have over-head exposed beams in your bedroom, the first thing to do would be paint them the same color as the ceiling, then per-form the invisibility ritual located in the remedies section in Chapter 1 on page 39.

The best rituals to perform in your bedroom are ones that relate to sleep, dreams, and of course, love.

There are six Star Runes that I have chosen to include in this room because so much of our lives are spent here, both waking and sleeping. Whatever your status: married, single, male, female, parent, or not, the following Star Runes include something for everyone. The first three have to do with waking and the last three with sleeping.

The first two should be viewed in the color green either by copying them onto green paper or by tracing the actual symbol in green.

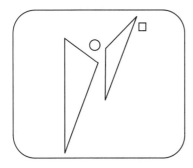

Figure 54. Health, Emotional Strength

Physical health is the best path to emotional strength. This Star Rune is a reminder that true wealth is achieved only when mind, body, and spirit are in balance.

Figure 55. Physical Strength, Motherhood, Goddess Energy, Balance of Opposites, Relationships With Women

To become a mother is to balance the apparent opposites of physical strength (worldly pursuits) with Goddess energy (spiritual and creative pursuits) thereby giving birth to all things possible. Our hopes and dreams must be planted within Mother Earth before they can grow.

The next Star Rune should be viewed in the color red either by copying it onto red paper or by tracing the actual symbol in red.

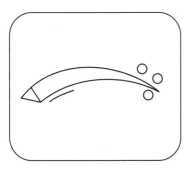

Figure 56. Fatherhood, God Energy, Relationships With Men, Sexual Energy

The relationships with men in our lives bring us a deeper understanding of the phrase "just do it." God energy is a powerful motivator inspiring us to reach out and acquire what we need in our lives, and to do so without hesitation.

We've seen the waking side, now for the sleeping side. The first Star Rune that has to do with sleeping should be viewed in the color light blue either by copying it onto light blue paper or by tracing the actual symbol in light blue.

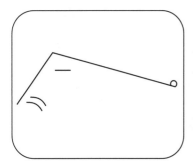

Figure 57. Dreams, Subconscious Mind

"To sleep. Perchance, to dream." Shakespeare said it best. Dreams are our subconscious minds communicating with us. To pay special attention to our dreams and the symbolism in our lives brings us closer to the core of our being. We must dream it before we can be it.

The second Star Rune having to do with sleep should be viewed in the color indigo either by copying it onto indigo paper or by tracing the actual symbol in indigo.

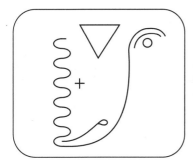

Figure 58. Mind, Reasoning, Attunement

The full power of the mind is beyond human comprehension. A few scratch the surface of our reasoning abilities, but attunement is the key to the full use of our minds. Only when we transcend our physical limitations can health truly be achieved. Our minds attune themselves and process the day's events through sleep.

The last Star Rune in the bedroom should only be used here if you are trying to conceive. If you don't want to be pregnant at this time, keep this Star Rune out of sight, especially in the bedroom. It should be viewed in the color orange either by copying it onto orange paper or by tracing the actual symbol in orange.

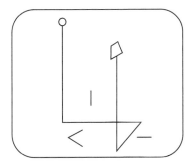

**Figure 59. Elements
of Creation, Conception**

When all of the elements of creation are present, they must be brought together in such a way that allows conception to take place. Simply having all the elements does not guarantee conception. Action and organization must also exist.

The Tarot Trump for this section is rather obvious—the Lovers. Even if you are single, the Lovers will help you bring partnerships into your life whether they are romantic or not.

Sweet dreams!

Bathroom—Clean It Up

You stumble out of bed every morning, make your way to the bathroom and switch on the light. After relieving your bladder, you shave, brush your teeth and hop in the shower. Combing through your wet hair, you begin to come alive and, while putting on your makeup, thoughts of the day to come are starting to run through your mind. One last look in the mirror before heading out the door and you are ready to greet the day. That night, you brush your teeth, wash your face, take one last look at yourself in the mirror, then go to bed.

The bathroom is the only room in the house that *always* reflects our image. We look at ourselves in various states of dress, undress, and dishevelment. The bathroom mirror reflects reality. Now isn't that a scary thought! It's also the place where we get clean. We may wash our hands in the kitchen sink, but the bathroom's primary purpose is cleansing—both inside and out. The bathroom, along with the kitchen, is the most essential room in the house and the one that we can't live without. Even an efficiency apartment has a bathroom even if it only has a hotplate for cooking. And just like the kitchen, it's extremely important to keep the bathroom clean.

If your bathroom is dark or poorly decorated, you see yourself in those surroundings literally, and picture yourself there figuratively. What a depressing way to start and end the day. Keep colors light and decorating simple in your bathroom. Colors of blue and green not only aid the flow of water, they aid digestion and promote good health. The use of reds and oranges should be kept to a minimum for they are Fire colors and Fire and Water do not mix. This is a room in which to relax. Decorate it as such. Stay away from busy patterns and if you must have reading material, make sure it's something you enjoy. Try not to catch up on work while in the bathroom!

The first thing to do in your bathroom every day is keep the toilet lid closed and make sure it is down before you flush. We have all heard the expression, "Flushing your (money, relationship, etc.) down the drain." There is a reason for that cliché. Chi is attracted to all that water and is easily pulled down the drain. Depending upon the locations of your bathroom(s), that could be precisely what is happening in your life. If your bathroom is in the Bagua area of Career, you may find it difficult to keep a job. If it's in the Bagua area of Fame and Reputation, you may find yourself the subject of nasty, and untrue, gossip.

There really is no good location in your home for bathrooms because bathrooms promote negative Chi flow. Think of them as whirlpools in the river of Chi. You can steer safely away from them, but they are a part of your house that you must have. The worst location for a bathroom in a two-story house is over the front door, for anyone entering your house is going to feel unclean. Bathroom energy also contaminates beneficial Chi entering the house. If you have a bathroom over the front door or sharing a wall with it you can use the crystal separation spell described on page 138.

Some Feng Shui practitioners recommend closing each drain after every use, but that's a pain. You can steer the Chi away from your drains by keeping live plants next to the sink and tub. Plants love bathrooms! All that moisture ensures that they will never die of thirst. Another way to keep the Chi moving is by placing mirrors on every wall. This also tends to brighten a dark bathroom. I don't mean floor to ceiling and wall to wall mirrors, although I've seen some bathrooms like that, but who wants to look at themselves when they are sitting on the toilet? Not me. I'm talking about small round mirrors like I discussed in Chapter 1. They bounce the Chi around the room and prevent it from going down the drain.

Many new houses these days are being built with a separate little room for the toilet. This is excellent Feng Shui. It keeps the worst of your waste contained. If your toilet is reflected in the mirror that you use every day, try to find a way to disguise it. Seeing the item we use to remove waste from our bodies in conjunction with our reflection is a negative association. A small screen or, better yet, a half-wall are elegant ways to solve this Feng Shui problem.

Along with keeping the toilet lid down, try to keep the bathroom door closed also, especially if the door is at the end of a hallway. This keeps positive Chi in the house and not going down the drain. Ideally, the door to any bathroom will be directly across from a solid wall and have at least one wall that is an outside wall to insure that waste is carried outside of the home. If your bathroom does not have a wall to the outside, do the following ritual. It will ensure that human waste is carried outside and doesn't get stuck in your house by creating a magickal screen over your sinks, tub, and toilets. This ritual also prevents beneficial Chi from being pulled down the drain minimizing the negative effect that bathrooms have on your house.

Screen Ritual

Perform this ritual for each toilet, sink, and tub in your house. Anything that has a drain. Don't forget the washing machine! This is also a good healing ritual, symbolically holding onto the cure while getting rid of the ailment.

TOOLS NEEDED:
Athame
Loose weave white or natural colored cloth
(cheesecloth works well)
Chalice with dark liquid (do not use wine or you will
flush your prosperity away, combine all the
different food colorings for a dark liquid effect)
A clear quartz crystal in Chalice (this represents
positive Chi)

Prepare yourself for ritual.
Invoke a Goddess and God of Water, Healing, or Menstruation. Believe it or not, there is a Goddess of toilets! Her name is Tsi-Ku.
Invoke the Water Element.
Stretch the cloth tightly over the sink, toilet, or drain, making sure that the weave is loose enough to allow the liquid through, but tight enough to hold onto the crystal.
Pour all the liquid down the drain until the chalice is empty and the crystal is caught on the cloth while saying the following:

*Negative Chi flows through this screen and down the
    drain.*
Out of this house, far away and without strain.
Positive Chi flows over this screen and stays.
Comfortable in my house every night and all the days.

It is done!

So Mote It Be!

Repeat for every drain in the house.
Thank and dismiss Water.
Thank and dismiss Goddess and God.
Thoroughly wash chalice, wash the cloth, then either bury
or dispose of the cloth. Don't burn it.
The ritual is ended.

Bathrooms are not a good place to perform any rituals
other than those directly related to a bathroom because of the
tendency of the energy to go down the drain.

Two Star Runes are appropriate in the bathroom. The first
one is obvious. The second, not so obvious. The first Star Rune
should be viewed in the color green either by copying it onto
green paper or by tracing the actual symbol in green.

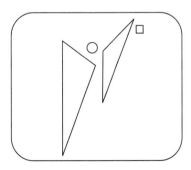

**Figure 60. Health,
Emotional Strength**

Physical health is the best path to
emotional strength. This Star Rune is
a reminder that true wealth is
achieved only when mind, body,
and spirit are in balance.

When I'm in the shower or on the toilet, with nothing to occupy my mind, it tends to wander. In such wanderings, solutions to problems are found. I finally had to get a divers chalkboard to put in the shower to write down all the ideas I have while showering, because once the water gets turned off those ideas tend to go down the drain (pun intended!). The point I want to make is that the solitude we experience while in the bathroom can be a mind expanding time if we are brave enough to act upon those ideas.

The second Star Rune for the bathroom should be viewed in the color red either by copying it onto red paper or by tracing the actual symbol in red.

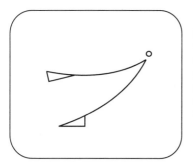

Figure 61. Courage, Bravery
Maintaining the courage of our convictions in the midst of others with the same beliefs is easy, but being aggressive and asserting our beliefs when we are alone in them makes us truly brave. This Star Rune helps us to keep our individuality.

The Moon hides those things we don't want others to see. It regulates our cycles and the natural rhythms of life making it the perfect Tarot trump for the bathroom.

Decorate your bathroom with items and colors that make you look good and feel good. That way, you see yourself surrounded by beauty every time you look in the mirror, and you carry this positive image of yourself into your waking and sleeping lives.

Home Office—Inspiration and Productivity

We all have work we need to do at home and with the advent of personal computers, nearly everyone spends some time sitting in front of that glowing screen. From playing solitaire to creating party invitations, surfing the Net and e-mailing loved ones, the computer has become a member of many families. From that perspective, it really should have its own room. I know this is not always possible. Whether your work space is a desk in the corner of your bedroom, the kitchen table, or a spare bedroom, it needs to be a space free of distractions and full of energy.

Desks, like beds and the stove, are primary power spots in your home. The placement of your desk is vital for the positive flow of Chi. You will always want to face your desk toward the door of the room so you are not startled by someone entering. Besides, having your back to an open door makes for a nervous, "always looking over your shoulder" mentality, which is the last thing you need when trying to get work done. It makes us feel as if there is always something going on behind our backs. If it is not possible to face the door from behind your desk, place a mirror on the wall in front of you that allows you to see the door.

Try to place your desk in the area of the room that is most appropriate to the type of work you are doing. For example, my desk is located in Wealth and Prosperity (North) facing Knowledge and Self-Cultivation (NorthEast). This puts my desk chair in Career (NorthWest). Since my career is as a full-time writer, this is a perfect setup for me. If you are a student, try the opposite and seat yourself in Knowledge and Self-Cultivation looking forward toward a future career. If most of the work done on your desk is creative in nature, place your desk in the East (Creativity and Children). This is also a good place for a child's desk as it allows them to fully express themselves.

The Health and Family, Love and Marriage, and Helpful People and Travel areas are *not* auspicious places for your desk. If you place your desk in one of these areas, you may find that your only companionship is coming from chat rooms and that you are neglecting relationships in your life.

Keep the Water element to a minimum in your office, as too much water will cause you to get too emotionally wrapped up in your work. If you have a fountain or fish tank, great, just make sure that they are not the primary focus in the room. Earth is best, tempered slightly with Fire. If you are having trouble staying put at your desk and find yourself distracted easily from your work, place a heavy grounding stone on your desk somewhere. An obsidian paperweight would be a good choice.

If you are finding yourself lacking energy, put a touch of Fire in the room. I have two inspiration candles that I burn while I'm working. One is dedicated to the Goddess Bridget for inspiration and healing (I find that writing is great therapy). The other one is dedicated to whatever current project I have under way. The one burning for this project is a rainbow-colored candle.

If lack of creativity or clear thought is your problem, try hanging wind chimes in a place that will sound them occasionally, like under a vent. Trust me, having wind chimes sounding constantly can get a little annoying. If wind chimes are not your cup of tea, try adding an object that has a yellow color. Even a favorite beanbag animal can magickally enhance your creativity.

Now for the hard part. Keep clutter to a minimum and your desk cleared off. Excuse me for a minute while I laugh hysterically. When I am working—like now—there are so many piles and papers on my desk that barely a square inch of wood shows through. I sometimes forget what color my desk is during the final stages of any project. The good news is that all these papers are directly related to the task at hand. I find it extremely annoying and a waste of time to put everything away in the evening only to get it all out again in the morning. Besides, I work at odd hours and when I wake up with an idea at three in the morning, I need to write it down then. If I spend too much time "getting organized" I lose the idea. Sometimes those ideas come back and sometimes they don't. All this to say, spread out and get messy if you want as long as you stay focused on one thing at a time.

If there are too many *different* projects on your desk at the same time, you may find yourself overwhelmed by the sheer volume of work and end up not even wanting to sit down and start *anything*. Keep a master list of all the projects that you are currently working on and keep *that* on your desk if you must. File away everything else that doesn't have to do with your current project. No filing cabinet? Try using baskets. Label each one with its specific project and stack them behind you. That way, you can tell at a glance where something is and pick it up at a moment's notice.

Speaking of baskets, "in" baskets are excellent Feng Shui, they not only keep papers organized, but they are also an indication of fresh ideas flowing into your life. Place your "in" basket on the North end of your desk to encourage wealth and prosperity. Your calculator is also a good enhancement in this area of your desk, because it shows that you are always adding wealth to your life.

Keep decorations simple and work-centered in this room. Inspirational posters or paintings that open your imagination just by staring at them are good choices. Photos of family are okay because they remind you of one of the reasons for your work, just don't fill the room with photos of family members or you may feel as though you are neglecting them.

If your home office is a desk in the corner of another room, try and find a way to partition it off, either with a screen, plants, or curtains. This keeps the work energy contained and keeps distractions to a minimum. Make a rule that when you are sitting at your desk, you are not to be disturbed unless it's an emergency. Close the door to your room; turn on music if you like. (I work better with music on, yet my husband says it distracts him when he is writing.) Wear headphones with nature sounds if you want to block out the world, but be careful about the music though, because if it is too soothing, you may find yourself nodding off over your keyboard!

Most important, this is a *work* area, treat it as such. Respect it and you'll get a lot of work done. If you must use the dining room or kitchen table as your desk, have a large basket available so you can easily stow all of your supplies. That way you can move your desk off the table at a moment's notice. A tablecloth designated for work is also a good idea. The act of placing the cloth on the table and setting out your working tools prepares your mind for work. Removing those items transforms the table back to its main purpose, nourishing the body and soul.

Rituals related to job changes, career, and wealth are enhanced when performed in your home office. If you work at home on a regular basis, the best Bagua areas for your home office are Career and Wealth and Prosperity. If your "office" is a sewing room or craft area, rituals involving creativity and inspiration are especially effective here and will be greatly enhanced if you are in the Creativity and Children Bagua area. Knowledge and Self-Cultivation is the best Bagua area for your office or desk if you are a student.

Since our home offices vary in scope from home to home, I am presenting a variety of Star Runes that can be used to enhance this area. Pick one, two, or all of them. The choice is yours.

The first Star Rune should be viewed in the color red either by copying it onto red paper or by tracing the actual symbol in red.

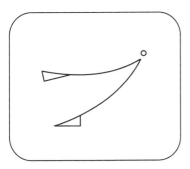

Figure 62. Courage, Bravery

Maintaining the courage of our convictions in the midst of others with the same beliefs is easy, but being aggressive and asserting our beliefs when we are alone in them makes us truly brave. This Star Rune helps us to keep our individuality.

The next Star Rune should be viewed in the color orange either by copying it onto orange paper or by tracing the actual symbol in orange.

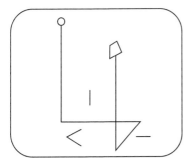

Figure 63. Elements of Creation, Conception

When all of the elements of creation are present, they must be brought together in such a way that allows conception to take place. Simply having all the elements does not guarantee conception. Action and organization must also exist.

The next Star Rune should be viewed in the color yellow either by copying it onto yellow paper or by tracing the actual symbol in yellow.

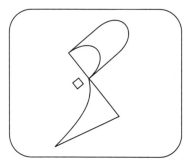

Figure 64. Power, Perpetual Motion

One of the great truths of the Universe is the saying (and I'm paraphrasing here): "Objects at rest or in motion tend to stay that way until acted upon by an outside force." That outside force doesn't have to be physical. We often need to ask for a push to get us going, whether from a spirit guide or from our own higher selves. And once we have motion, it becomes perpetual, constantly renewing our power. Start that creativity flowing and it will extend itself into all the areas of life.

The next two Star Runes should be viewed in the color light blue either by copying them onto light blue paper or by tracing the actual symbol in light blue.

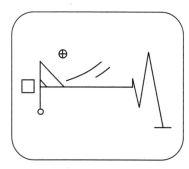

Figure 65. Multisource Information

Information from only one source always leaves us with a skewed perspective. Wading through and disseminating information from many different sources brings us closer to truth and understanding. If you are feeling overwhelmed with too many projects, focus on this Star Rune to help you break down massive amounts of information.

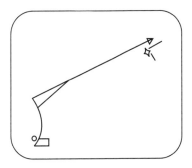

Figure 66. Service to Others, Speaking Out, Justice

True justice lies not in others or in a governmental system. True justice lies in speaking out our truths, whatever they may be, without attachment to the final outcome. In this way, we truly serve others and ourselves. For courage in speaking your mind to others, use this Star Rune as a focus.

The last two Star Runes for the home office should be viewed in the color indigo either by copying them onto indigo paper or by tracing the actual symbol in indigo.

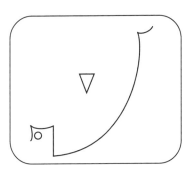

Figure 67. Third Eye, Clarity

The third eye increases our ability to see beyond the physical and into the spiritual. Clarity of purpose opens our minds to true intellect. Opening the third eye, we see beyond the limitations of the body and see beyond our masks and embrace true understanding.

Figure 68. Mind, Reasoning, Attunement

The full power of the mind is beyond human comprehension. A few scratch the surface of our reasoning abilities, but attunement is the key to the full use of our minds. Only when we transcend our physical limitations can understanding truly be achieved.

We must sacrifice certain things in our lives in order to obtain others so the Hanged Man is the Tarot trump for the home office. In this case, it is a sacrifice of time and energy in exchange for material wealth and satisfaction in our work. A sense of purpose is inherent in this card.

Your home office is all about inspiration and productivity. If you are someone like me who works entirely out of the home, it can be one of the most important rooms in your house. If, instead, you use your home office or desk more for play and creative endeavors, the importance dims, but not much. Play is just as important as work. Even more so, sometimes. Our work enables us to have the time and money to play. Play with this space.

Closets, Attics, and Basements—
Hidden Opportunities

The closet monster; cobwebs in the attic; basement fears. These three places have inspired more Hollywood horror movies than Stephen King. I believe there is a reason. These spaces in our homes represent the darker corners of our own psyches as well as memories of the past and seldom-used items of the present. Think about it. Other than the closet that you keep your everyday clothes in, what lurks in the dark spaces of your home?

Under the heading of seldom-used items of the present, there's the coat closet—seasonal; holiday decorations in the attic—also seasonal; tools in the basement—hobby time; craft supplies in the basement—also hobby time; cleaning supplies in the hall closet—necessary, but only occasionally.

Memories of the past include photo albums in the hall closet—fun, but how often do you look at them? Your wedding dress in the attic—put away for sentimental reasons and future generations. A broken toaster in the basement—yes you could probably fix it, but when? Old yearbooks and love letters from college in the attic—trips down memory lane.

Then we get into the darker parts of our own minds. What person reading this was not afraid of the closet monster when he or she was little? If you raised your hand, you are definitely in the minority. To this day it is hard for me to sleep with the closet door even partially open. Feng Shui has an explanation for this: unfamiliar shapes seen when you are half-asleep can startle you (as I talked about in the section on bedrooms earlier in this chapter). There is also the mess to consider. I know of no one who keeps a perfectly well-ordered and organized closet. Keeping your closet doors closed solves these problems quite handily.

Even expressions point to attics as the repositories of our minds: "She has bats in her belfry." "His elevator doesn't go all the way to the top." "I need to clear these cobwebs out of my head."

On the other hand, basements represent our fears. Depression is typically referred to as "being down in the dumps." Panic creeps up on us from the pit of our stomachs and fear has often been described as "a sinking feeling."

As Witches, we are constantly exploring and expanding every aspect of our surroundings and ourselves including the darker sides. These places in our homes need exploration and airing out as well. You may find that a thorough attic cleaning is just what you need to get rid of mental blocks in your life. The same "use it, or lose it" principle applies here. It's easy to relegate our problems to the unseen areas of the house where we tend to forget about them. Don't do it. If you don't intend to fix that toaster this week then give it away! Get it out of the house. Trust me, you'll feel better. Your home won't be cluttered

with non-working items and you won't feel guilty every time
you look at it. "I really need to fix that this weekend," becomes
a burden you can do without!

These spaces also represent past lives, memories that we
carry with us and "white elephants" or karmic debts that weigh
us down. Another important reason to keep these areas cleaned
out and clutter free. I actually did a scrying ritual in a closet one
time. Talk about scary! The purpose of the ritual was to see the
dark faces within me. It worked—almost too well! Any ritual
involving facing fears or reliving past lives can be done in these
dark places. You will be amazed at the signals that get through!

The following Star Runes will help you explore those
darker areas within your home and within yourself. The first
one should be viewed in the color red either by copying it onto
red paper or by tracing the actual symbol in red.

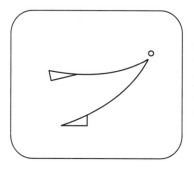

Figure 69. Courage, Bravery
Maintaining the courage of our convictions in the midst of others with
the same beliefs is easy, but being
aggressive and asserting our beliefs
when we are alone in them makes
us truly brave. This Star Rune helps
us to keep our individuality.

The second Star Rune should be viewed in the color green
either by copying it onto green paper or by tracing the actual
symbol in green.

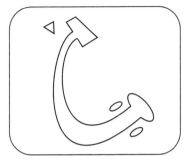

**Figure 70. Self-Love, Going
Within, Inner Quiet**

We must have self-love in order to
give love to others. Only by going
within and finding the dance within
the stillness can we achieve the inner
quiet that is vital to love.

The third Star Rune should be viewed in the color light
blue either by copying it onto light blue paper or by tracing the
actual symbol in light blue.

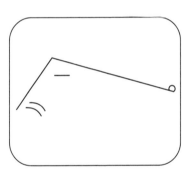

**Figure 71. Dreams,
Subconscious Mind**

"To sleep. Perchance, to dream."
Shakespeare said it best. Dreams are
our subconscious minds communicating with us. Paying special attention to our dreams and the
symbolism in our lives brings us
closer to the core of our being. We
must dream it before we can be it.

The last Star Rune for our hidden spaces should be viewed
in the color purple either by copying it onto purple paper or by
tracing the actual symbol in purple.

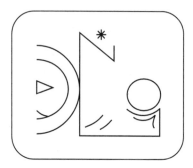

Figure 72. Self-Integration, Understanding the Complexities of the Human Condition

By understanding others, we better understand ourselves. In the most complex forms lie the simplest equations. Integrating these ideas within ourselves combines and joins us to each other and, in essence, melds us with the Universe as a whole.

The Wheel of Fortune is the most prominent Tarot card here because it brings to mind responsibilities not necessarily of our own making—that damn toaster again! And hidden opportunities springing from past lives—that old painting you bought from that starving artist in college could now be worth something!

Any way you choose to look at it, the closets, attics, and basements in our lives need to be as clear as the rest of our homes. Sort. Clean out. Throw away. Recycle. You'll feel so much better afterward.

Patios, Balconies, and Yards— Outdoor Sanctuaries

Ah, summertime. Warm weather. Vacations. Outdoor living. Sitting in a lawn chair listening to the sounds of a summer evening. Kids playing in the yard. A lawn mower down the street. Watching the lightning bugs start to appear as the sun goes down. Sipping a cool beverage and reveling in Nature at Her finest.

Whether your outdoor space is fifty acres of private land or a planterbox on your windowsill, enjoying the great outdoors is one of the main reasons most of us became Witches in the first place. We see all of Nature as sacred whether the Goddess is dressed in Her silvery white winter cloak or in the blossoms of midsummer.

There are so many schools of thought regarding gardens and the great outdoors that I could devote an entire book to the subject. On the other hand, gardening is such a personal endeavor that it is difficult to make any suggestions at all. What it really comes down to is that there are very few "hard and fast" rules about the great outdoors in traditional Feng Shui and Wiccan Feng Shui could make it into a high art! Then again, traditional Oriental gardens are methodically laid out and planned down to the smallest detail. All this to say, that this section is shorter than the others for the reasons listed above.

When planning your yard and garden, keep these tips in mind:

- Trees are protectors and are best kept to the rear of the house. Just make sure that they don't overshadow your front door or the Chi may have difficulty finding its way inside.
- Keep pathways curved and avoid sharp angles so that the Chi flows easily.
- Fountains, ponds, and pools are excellent Feng Shui if kept clean and free of debris.
- Vary the shapes and sizes of the plants and immediately remove dead or diseased plants.

All rituals are enhanced by doing them in the great outdoors!

The Star Runes for the great outdoors encourage health and growth. The first two should be viewed in the color green either by copying them onto green paper or by tracing the actual symbol in green.

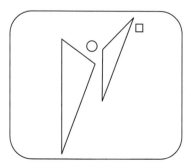

Figure 73. Health, Emotional Strength

Physical health is the best path to emotional strength. This Star Rune is a reminder that true wealth is achieved only when mind, body, and spirit are in balance.

Figure 74. Physical Strength, Motherhood, Goddess Energy, Balance of Opposites, Relationships With Women

To become a mother is to balance the apparent opposites of physical strength (worldly pursuits) with Goddess energy (spiritual and creative pursuits) thereby giving birth to all things possible. Our hopes and dreams must be planted within Mother Earth before they can grow.

The next two Star Runes should be viewed in the color yellow either by copying them onto yellow paper or by tracing the actual symbol in yellow.

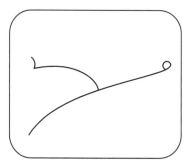

Figure 75. Trust, Openness

In opening ourselves to the power inherent in the Universe, we trust ourselves to make the right decisions in life. In trusting others, we learn the most important lesson—both from loyalty and from betrayal—that we must remain open.

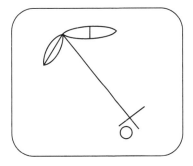

Figure 76. Growth, Expansion
The seed lies dormant waiting for the earth to warm before it can grow. Roots spring forth, hidden from the world, prior to the expansion that will break through the ground and bring us ever closer to the light of truth. Nurture creativity and it will always grow.

The Sun is the Tarot trump that shines upon us in our outdoor spaces reminding us of our innocent natures and that we are all Her children.

Kept natural or dramatically landscaped, your garden should be a place of retreat when the world gets to be too much. Fill it with plants and statuary that give you pleasure. Relax, put your feet up, sip a cool margarita and read a book. In your garden, you can stop the world and get off for a while.

Temple Space—Perfect Balance

If you are fortunate enough to have a permanent space dedicated as a temple, good for you! You are in a very small group of people. Needless to say, this is one area of your home you must decorate according to your own tradition. I only have two suggestions for this space: that all the elements present be in perfect balance and that you not enter this space unless you are preparing for or doing a magickal working or meditation. If you find yourself retreating to this space only for privacy or after arguments, energies of those types will begin to build up and affect the space, and it's important that this space be clear for magickal workings.

You could put all the Star Runes in your temple space and meditate upon them at will. They would strengthen your magickal workings and rituals and make the room vibrate with power. This may be too much for some of you, however, so I have chosen six that are directly related to magickal and personal growth.

The first two should be viewed in the color yellow either by copying them onto yellow paper or by tracing the actual symbol in yellow.

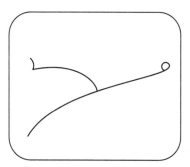

Figure 77. Trust, Openness

In opening ourselves to the power inherent in the Universe, we trust ourselves to make the right decisions in life. In trusting others, we learn the most important lesson—both from loyalty and from betrayal—that we must remain open.

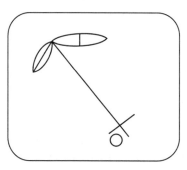

Figure 78. Growth, Expansion

The seed lies dormant waiting for the earth to warm before it can grow. Roots spring forth, hidden from the world, prior to the expansion that will break through the ground and bring us ever closer to the light of truth.

The next Star Rune should be viewed in the color indigo either by copying it onto indigo paper or by tracing the actual symbol in indigo.

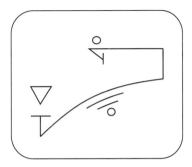

Figure 79. Navigation, Direction, Future Map, Guidance, "Coming Home"

Without direction and maps, we quickly lose our way and wander without purpose. Navigation and guidance, be it from within or without, allows us to find our way home to the bosom of our families.

The following two Star Runes should be viewed in the color purple either by copying them onto purple paper or by tracing the actual symbol in purple.

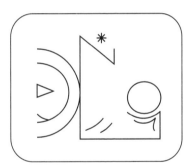

Figure 80. Self-Integration, Understanding the Complexities of the Human Condition

By understanding others, we better understand ourselves. In the most complex forms lie the simplest equations. Integrating these ideas within ourselves combines and joins us to each other and, in essence, melds us with the universe as a whole.

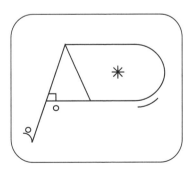

Figure 81. Teaching, Bringing Others to a Spiritual Home

The best teachers bring others to a spiritual home. It matters less what home that is than that the students find a way that completes them. Setting another's feet upon a path is a noble and rewarding vocation. We are all teachers in our own way, even if we never see the fruits of our labors. Each path is complete within itself.

The last Star Rune for the Temple area should be viewed in the color white. A pearlized white on a black background is the most powerful way to display this symbol. Choose a color if you prefer. Just make sure that the color *truly* represents what you wish to learn.

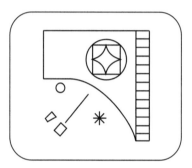

Figure 82. Balance

Justice is the Tarot trump for this area. The scales of balance are constantly in motion and the Lady who holds them weighs us all without prejudice and with open arms and love.

Enjoy this space. You may find yourself sending tendrils of the energy from this space into different areas of your home. One of the great things about being a High Priestess is that my home gets to benefit from the energy of the entire group. Treat this sacred space with reverence and respect and they will return to your home three-fold.

4

WRITTEN IN THE STARS

We've discussed the great circle of life. We've discussed the elements of the planet on which we live. We've discussed every room in your house. We've discussed stones, animals, colors, and a wide assortment of enhancements. Now it is time to discuss the otherworldly associations of Tarot, Star Runes, and Astrology and how they fit in with Wiccan Feng Shui.

Tarot and the Bagua

Now that you have a working knowledge of the trumps and suits within the Tarot, it is time to put that knowledge to some practical use. I know, I said that you did not have to know how to read Tarot in order to use it in Wiccan Feng Shui. That hasn't changed, but for those of you who would like to use it, try the spread in Figure 83.

Each card in this spread relates to that Bagua area in your life. Lay out the circle either widdershins or deosil depending

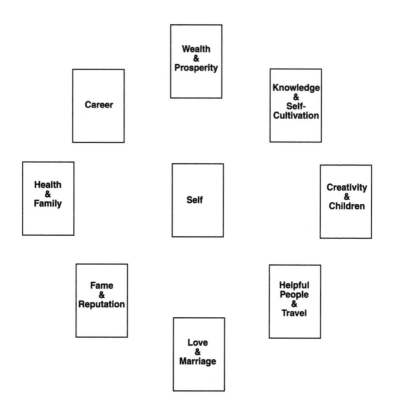

Figure 83. Feng Shui Tarot Spread

on what you are asking. One card in each position gives you a greater understanding of what is going on in your life at this moment. Placing three cards in each position is a great way to do a life reading for the past, present, and future because each aspect of your life is represented.

Star Runes and the Bagua

Casting the Star Runes is similar to casting other runes. You can make your own set of Star Runes by copying them onto colored paper or carving them onto wooden disks.

Since the Star Runes came to me three dimensionally, and they can be read from any angle, there are no reversed or "negative" readings.

Use as many or as few Star Runes as you think necessary. Numerology is an effective force in all types of divination so use the following guide to determine the scope of your reading or simply use your intuition to determine the number of Star Runes you use. The best method is ultimately your choice.

1 = Health and Family (a quick answer, or a question about a beginning)

2 = Love and Marriage (a partnership or love issue)

3 = Creativity and Children (a growth issue, children, or a past/present/future insight into a specific area)

4 = Wealth and Prosperity (questions about home, stability, and foundations)

5 = Knowledge and Self-Cultivation (questions about major changes and upheavals)

6 = Helpful People and Travel (questions about relationships in general, be they lover, family or friends)

7 = Fame and Reputation (issues of a spiritual nature)

8 = Career (money and power issues)

9 = Endings or issues that need to be brought to completion

You can also choose a specific rune for personal work. Say, for example, that you are moving to a new town or changing jobs and are worried about making new friends. Write down your worries and concerns on a piece of paper, then take the relationship building rune (see Figure 38) and place it on the paper. If it's a new town, place the paper and the Star Rune on a map of the area in the Helpful People and Travel Bagua area. If it's a new job, do the same thing using a Career rune and place it on your desk or in the Career Bagua area. You could use the numerology mentioned above as to the number of days you keep them in the Bagua areas or you could simply use your intuition.

Since the Star Runes came to me in my dreams, they are especially potent when used for Dreamwork. If you are having trouble remembering your dreams, or perhaps you simply want to begin an intensive Dreamwork session, you can place the Star Rune for dreams, subconscious mind (see Figure 57) under your pillow. I don't recommend that you do this more than once a week or you may have trouble waking. You might also awake tired from your nighttime travels. When you use the Star Runes in Dreamwork try to arrange for a day off the next day so you can assimilate the dream information. All the Star Runes can be used in this way, but remember this is the Star Rune at its *most* powerful, so be careful.

Experiment with the Star Runes. I am sure you will find ways to use them that I have not even dreamt of (pun intended). Remember, the Star Runes are much more than a Wiccan Feng Shui or divination tool. They are a path to follow to help us achieve greater understanding of ourselves and the Universe around us.

Astrology and the Bagua

You may have wondered why I waited so late in the book to bring up the subject of astrology instead of including it in every chapter like I did with Tarot and the Star Runes. The answer is quite simple really. Most of the astrological signs straddle two

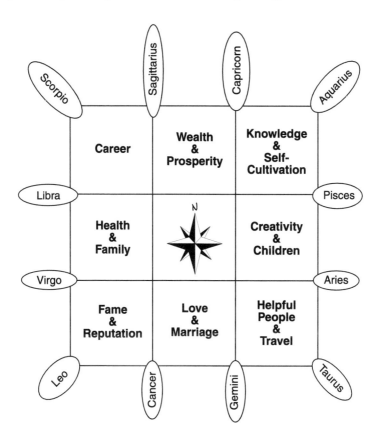

Figure 84. Astrological Bagua Map

Bagua areas and, because of this, it would have been confusing to devote a chapter to each sign and most of the signs did not fit within specific chapters. Besides, astrology is such a complex study that I hesitate to apply only surface meanings to the associations shown, even though every major newspaper in the country does so every day. But I never claimed to be a journalist, only a writer.

I've included this Bagua map simply as another possible layer to the arrangement of your home. What better way to find a room of your own than to discover where your astrological sign is located! For the astrologers amongst you, have fun!

5

SUMMATION

"Alexandria to Dragon Air Traffic Control. Coming in for a landing. Thank you for flying with Dragon Rider Decor. Think of us the next time you need to travel to the world of Wiccan Feng Shui. Enjoy your stay here at home and remember, the more you fly with us, the smoother the ride!"

It's true! The more you use Wiccan Feng Shui in your home, the easier it becomes to balance all aspects of your life. We have broken the chains of old thought and are being reborn into a new way of thinking. The Tarot trump of Judgment shows us releasing ourselves from the old patterns that restrict our growth.

Now we are free to receive all of what the Tarot trump of the World has to offer. The following House Blessing Ritual is the icing on the cake and the whipped cream on the Bagua areas of your house, pulling together all the enhancements and remedies into one sweet dish!

House Blessing Ritual

This ritual should be done when all the members of the household can be present. You could even make it a community affair in conjunction with a house-warming party. Choose a Goddess and a God of protection, home, comfort, or ask your patron Goddess and God to be present. Any time of the day or night is appropriate for this ritual as is any phase of the moon or any season. We cannot always plan what time of year we must move and this ritual is best done as soon as you move in. It can be done either before or after the consecration of each Bagua area. If done before, you will find yourself working in a sacred space from day one. If done after, your enhancements will receive yet another layer of consecration.

Give each person who lives in the home a role to play in this ritual. If others are present it is up to you whether or not you want them to play an active role. Everyone who participates will add a little bit of his or her energy to your home so choose carefully.

If you wish to use a Star Rune in this ritual use the one for balance (see Figure 85, below). It should be viewed in the color white. A pearlized white on a black background is the

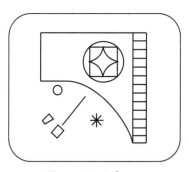

Figure 85. Balance

most powerful way to display this symbol. You can choose a color if you prefer, just make sure that the color *truly* represents what you wish to learn. Carve it into the bread or stir it into the wine.

I will be presenting this ritual with the Goddess Hestia and the God Osiris. Please feel free to change these to deities you work well with. The direction you move around the circle should be in accordance with your own tradition. Since I moved widdershins through the Bagua areas, I will move deosil through this ritual.

TOOLS NEEDED:

Athame

Representations of each element off your main altar:
    Incense for Air
    Red candle for Fire
    Water bowl or shell for Water
    Saucer of salt for Earth

Wine in chalice

Bread

Two white candles (one should be from your old
    home, lit there before you left. This transfers the
    energy from your old home to your new.)

Prepare yourself as you would for any magickal working and prepare the space according to your traditions.

Light the candle brought from your old home.

Facing East, call the element of Air to be present in the incense, and say:

Guardians of the East,
Powers of Air,
Be with me to bless and consecrate this home and keep this
    dwelling alive with the power of freshness and new
    beginnings.

The light of your creation, freshness, and clarity permeates this space. Burn bright in my home for now and evermore.

Walk through every room in the house with the smoke from the incense then walk the outside perimeter of your new home and yard. Make this procession one in which each person present is talking to the element of Air and telling it what they wish it to provide for the home. Return to main altar, and say:

This home is blessed and consecrated with the Power of Air.
So Mote It Be!

Facing South, call the element of Fire to be present in the red candle, and say:

Guardians of the South,
Powers of Fire,
Be with me to bless and consecrate this home and keep this dwelling alive with the power of Fire and the warmth of the Summer sun.
The light of your inspiration, courage, and love permeates this space.
Burn bright in my home for now and evermore.

Walk through every room in the house with the red candle, then walk the outside perimeter of your new home and yard. Make this procession one in which each person present is talking to the element of Fire and telling it what they wish it to provide for the home. Return to main altar, and say:

This home is blessed and consecrated with the Fire of the South.
So Mote It Be!

Facing West, call the element of Water to be present in the water bowl or shell, and say:

Guardians of the West,
Powers of Water,
Be with me to bless and consecrate this home and keep this
*   dwelling alive with the power of still and flowing*
*   waters.*
The light of your purity, health, and love permeates this
*   space.*
Burn bright in my home for now and evermore.

Walk through every room in the house with the water, sprinkling drops as you go, then walk the outside perimeter of your new home and yard. Make this procession one in which each person present is talking to the element of Water and telling it what they wish it to provide for the home. Return to main altar, and say:

This home is blessed and consecrated with the Water of the
*   West.*
So Mote It Be!

Facing North, call the element of Earth to be present in the salt, and say:

Guardians of the North,
Powers of Earth,
Be with me to bless and consecrate this home and keep this
*   dwelling alive with the power of the forest and fields.*
The light of your strength, stability, fertility, and growth
*   permeates this space.*
Burn bright in my home for now and evermore.

Walk through every room in the house with the salt, sprinkling it as you go, then walk the outside perimeter of your new home and yard. Make this procession one in which each person present is talking to the element of Earth and telling it what they wish it to provide for the home. Return to main altar, and say:

> *This home is blessed and consecrated with the salt of the*
> *   Earth.*
> *So Mote It Be!*

Facing North, invoke the Goddess and God asking them to be with you as you consecrate your new home, and say:

> *Hestia, Goddess of Home and Hearth*
> *Bless and consecrate this home and keep this dwelling alive*
> *   with your presence, love, and understanding.*
> *Hold us to your breast and fold us in your arms.*
> *Protect us from those who wish us harm.*
> *Be they of this world or beyond.*
> *So Mote It Be!*

> *Osiris, All-seeing God of this life and the next.*
> *Bless and consecrate this home and keep this dwelling alive*
> *   with your presence, love, and understanding.*
> *Hold us to your breast and fold us in your arms.*
> *Protect us from those who wish us harm.*
> *Be they of this world or beyond.*
> *So Mote It Be!*

With the candle brought from your old home light the new candle, and say:

> *I transfer all the positive energy from my old home to this*
> *   new home.*
> *So Mote It Be!*

Share the bread with everyone present. (Be sure to save some of the bread to offer to the Goddess and God.) And say:

We will never know hunger.
So Mote It Be!

Share the wine with everyone present. (Be sure to save some of the wine to offer to the Goddess and God.) And say:

We will never know thirst.
So Mote It Be!
May Joy and Prosperity Reign within this home!
So Mote It Be!

Thank and dismiss the elements.
Thank and dismiss the Goddess and God.
The ritual is ended.

After the ritual have a great feast to celebrate your new home. If you have a fireplace, use this candle to light the first fire within it. Then let both the new and old candles burn until they go out on their own. Take that little bit of bread and wine left over and offer it to the spirits of the yard or leave it on your front stoop to honor your ancestors, or both.

Blessed Be!

.

Quick Reference Guides

This section is here to give you a quick and easy way to look up enhancements for each Bagua area. Make copies of specific pages and take them with you while shopping for your home.

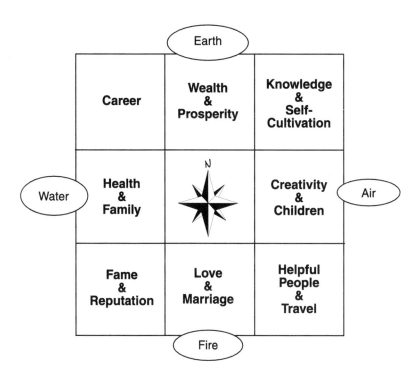

Figure 86. Elements

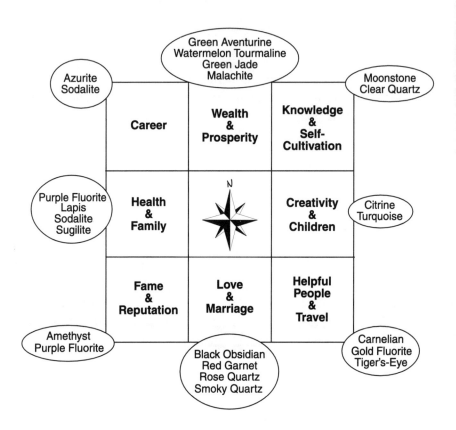

Figure 87. Stones

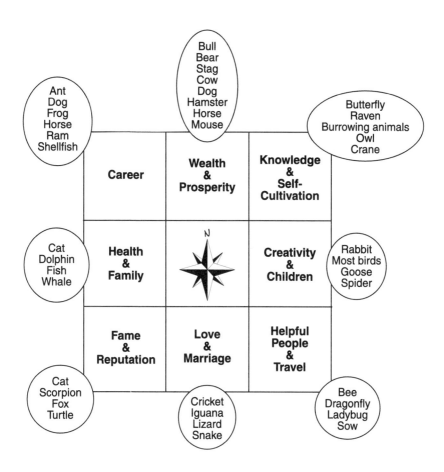

Figure 88. Animals

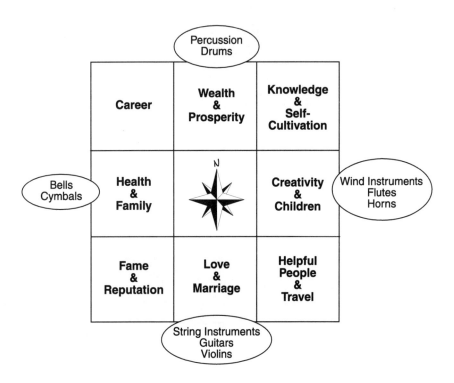

Figure 89. Musical Instruments

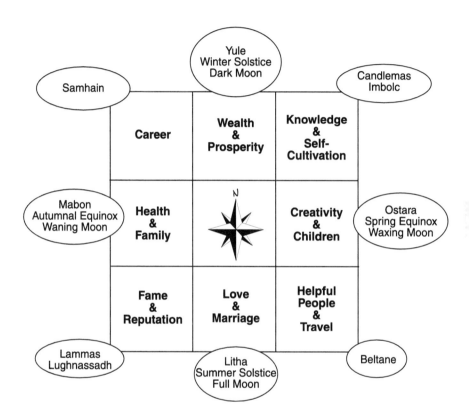

Figure 90. Sabbats—Solar/Lunar Phases

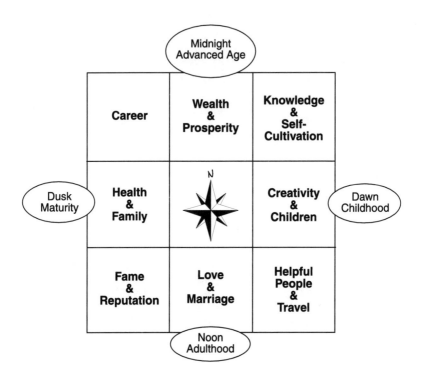

Figure 91. Times and Ages

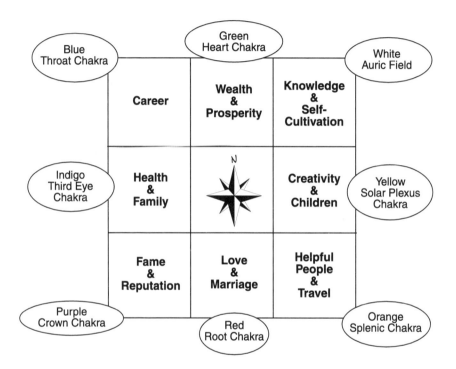

Figure 92. Colors and Chakras

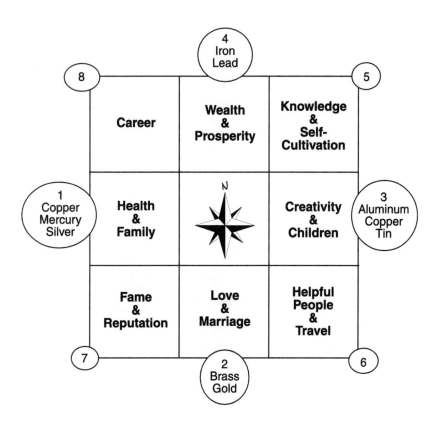

Figure 93. Numbers and Metals

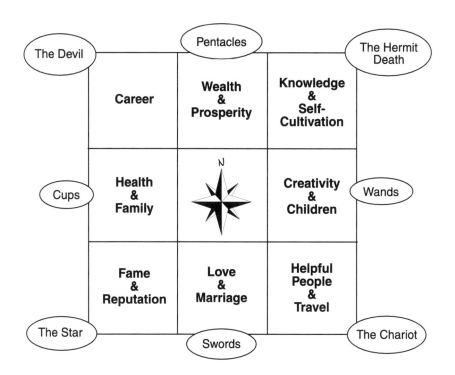

Figure 94. Tarot

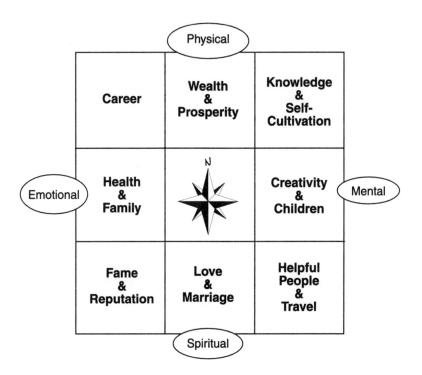

Figure 95. Planes

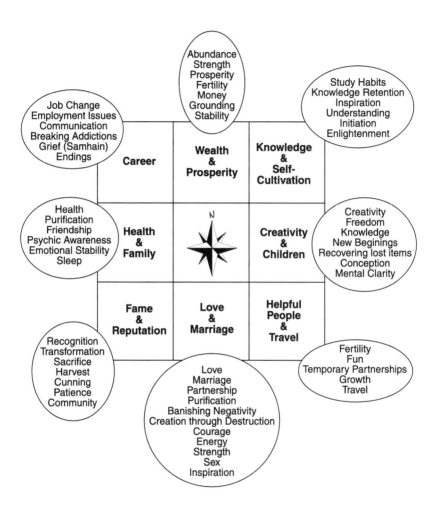

Abundance
Strength
Prosperity
Fertility
Money
Grounding
Stability

Study Habits
Knowledge Retention
Inspiration
Understanding
Initiation
Enlightenment

Job Change
Employment Issues
Communication
Breaking Addictions
Grief (Samhain)
Endings

Career

**Wealth
&
Prosperity**

**Knowledge
&
Self-
Cultivation**

Health
Purification
Friendship
Psychic Awareness
Emotional Stability
Sleep

**Health
&
Family**

N

**Creativity
&
Children**

Creativity
Freedom
Knowledge
New Beginings
Recovering lost items
Conception
Mental Clarity

**Fame
&
Reputation**

**Love
&
Marriage**

**Helpful
People
&
Travel**

Recognition
Transformation
Sacrifice
Harvest
Cunning
Patience
Community

Love
Marriage
Partnership
Purification
Banishing Negativity
Creation through Destruction
Courage
Energy
Strength
Sex
Inspiration

Fertility
Fun
Temporary Partnerships
Growth
Travel

Figure 96. Rituals

Pantheon

The following is a list and brief explanation of the gods and goddesses that have been presented throughout this book. You will find that several of them defy the traditional definition of a god or goddess. Some are heroes while still others are historical figures. It is my belief that what you need matters more than if that figure is a "real" god or goddess. We humans create our deities in our own image, so if a certain aspect of a person is what we need in our lives, who's to say that person cannot become a deity to us? Most pantheons have within them deities who were, at one time, human. And who's to say that becoming Divine is not the next step in our evolution? Certainly not me! All this to say, here is a nontraditional list of gods and goddesses.

Al-Lat: Al-Lat is the feminine aspect of the god Allah. Her name in Arabic simply means Goddess. Like many other goddesses, she is the central figure—the Mother—of a trinity. Al-Uzza represents the Maiden and Menat, the Crone. Her shrine was close to the holy city of Mecca where she appeared before her naked worshippers as a pillar of white granite. She is the embodiment of the desert at its most giving.

Amergin: The epic poem "I Am the Stag of Seven Tines" is attributed to this great bard. Many of us find our Mysteries inherent within that work. Amergin held great power with the gods, being able to grant wishes to even the leaders of the Tuatha De Danann (a race of divine beings). His creativity was instrumental in the establishment of many of the myths of ancient Ireland.

Artemis: This "Lady of the Beasts" is said to protect all of the animals of the forest—even the human ones! She is the Virgin Huntress who ensures that pregnant animals and their young are not hunted. She can be fierce in her duties, using her bow against any intruder. She is the goddess that pregnant women call upon to help them through the pain of childbirth.

Boann: When she approached the well of Segais, it rose up and drowned Boann. No one, not even goddesses were allowed to eat the fruit of the nine hazelnut trees that surrounded the well. The water could not return to its source, so it became the River Boyne and Boann became a goddess.

Bran: The legend and stories about Bran are long and involved. Suffice it to say that He is a god of the waning year and a fierce protector.

Brigid: Brigid was Goddess of Fire long before she was Christianized into a saint. From her cauldron of inspiration sprang forth the art of smithcraft, whistling, and poetry. Her abilities to heal included the invention of keening, designed to ease the grief she felt at the death of her son.

Cernunnos: The consort of the Great Mother, Cernunnos is the Lord of the Hunt. He is the Great Horned God bearing the antlers of the stag.

Deborah: Deborah was a Hebrew prophet and poetess. She sat in the open air beneath an olive tree and dispensed judgments. A charismatic leader, she not only raised an army but acted as its general as well.

Epona: Ancient Celtic rituals of sovereignty may have included a rite of marriage with this horse goddess. She was the sacred mare and as such brought dreams, both pleasant and unpleasant. The English word "nightmare" is derived from her Irish name, Mare.

Flora: This ancient Roman goddess was the queen of all plants. She was the embodiment of the flowers of springtime. Her worship was orgiastic in nature and the best way to honor her was to make love to anyone who happened to pass by.

Gonlod: This Scandinavian goddess of poetry was the original owner of the Cauldron of Inspiration before it was stolen by the God Odin.

Hestia: Hestia is a Greek goddess of home and hearth said to be the oldest of the goddesses of Olympia. Her form is seen in the flames of the hearth and new homes were considered incomplete until she was invoked by the lighting of the fire.

Kore: The fragrant breezes of springtime follow this goddess wherever she goes. She is the Maiden of the Earth and the buds of fresh growth.

Lugh: Lugh is often referred to as "the shining one" and "the long armed." He is a protector of the weak and is closely associated with grain. Because of this association, he is considered to sacrifice himself at the festival of first harvest. The festival of Lughnassadh is named after the god Lugh.

Mercury: This Greek god of communication is often shown with wings on his feet.

Osiris: An Egyptian god, Osiris was the counterpart of Isis. Because of his death and subsequent resurrection he is a god of this world and the next. His all-seeing eye protects and watches over us.

Pan: A Greek god of the woods and wild places, Pan celebrates life with wild abandon. Passion and fun are the words that best describe this playful god.

Selene: This Greek Moon goddess was married to the Sun, but had an earthly lover. She was said to be visiting this lover when she left the sky once a month.

Sithehenn: A Druidic prophet, Sithehenn foretold who would become the next High King of Ireland. He is closely associated with smithcraft, fire, and the consecration of tools.

Thoth: An Egyptian god of reincarnation, Thoth is said to be God of the Wise with an express interest in the sciences.

Tsi-Ku: A Chinese goddess of the outhouse who can foretell the future.

Bibliography

The following is a list of books that were instrumental in the writing of *Wiccan Feng Shui*. Compared to the sheer number of books I have read over the years that relate directly to this subject, this list is woefully short, but to list all of the books in my reference library would be a book unto itself. There is no way to know which have influenced me over the years. The books I have chosen to list below are ones that I referred to more than once during this project.

Adler, Margot. *Drawing Down the Moon*. Boston: Beacon Press, 1979.

Carr-Gomm, Philip and Stephanie. *The Druid Animal Oracle*. New York: Simon & Schuster, 1994.

Collins, Terah Kathryn. *The Western Guide to Feng Shui*. Carlsbad, Cal.: Hay House, 1996.

Cunningham, Scott. *Cunningham's Encyclopedia of Magical Herbs*. St. Paul, Minn.: Llewellyn Publications, 1985.

Gardner, Joy. *Color and Crystals*. Freedom, Cal.: The Crossing Press, 1988.

Lagatree, Kirsten M. *Feng Shui*. New York: Villard Books, 1996.

Lingerman, Hal A. *The Book of Numerology*. York Beach, Me.: Samuel Weiser, 1994.

McCoy, Edain. *Celtic Myth and Magick*. St. Paul, Minn.: Llewellyn Publications, 1995.

Monaghan, Patricia. *The Book of Goddesses and Heroines*. St. Paul, Minn.: Llewellyn Publications, 1989.

Paterson, Jacqueline Memory. *Tree Wisdom*. London: Thorsons, 1996.

Paungger, Johanna and Thomas Poppe. *Moon Time*. New York: Barnes & Noble Books, 1995.

Starhawk. *The Spiral Dance*. San Francisco: Harper Collins, 1979.

Stein, Diane. *The Women's Spirituality Book*. St. Paul, Minn.: Llewellyn Publications, 1987.

Webster, Richard. *101 Feng Shui Tips for the Home*. St. Paul, Minn.: Llewellyn Publications, 1998.

Wolfe, Amber. *In the Shadow of the Shaman*. St. Paul, Minn.: Llewellyn Publications, 1988.

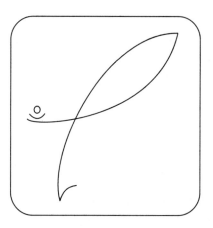

Figure 97. End

Index